The J-Dog Journey

Where is life?
Sometimes you have to go a long way
to discover who you are.

by

Kent R. Hunter

Church Doctor Ministries
Corunna, Indiana

Dedicated to my fellow Kingdom crazies:

Steve
Jason
Shelly H.
Tracee
Olive
Neil
JZ
Josh
Chris
Beth
Katie
Shelley S.
Adam
Mike
bff JC

TABLE OF CONTENTS

Chapter One
Sleeping

You know what I like about sleeping? You don't have to think about anything. I don't have to wonder about our next football game – and whether the coach will let me play. I don't have to think about Sarah. I am not sure what attracts me to her, anyway. She's okay. I guess. Maybe…for now. I don't even have to think about school. After three years and two months, I am ready for…I don't know what. I can't figure out why I'm on this earth. What's my purpose? I don't have to think about that.

I'll miss football. I like the challenge. I like lifting weights. I know, I'm a little crazy. I really like my fraternity brothers. These guys are family. Nobody judges anybody. I know I like the parties. The girls. The beer. I guess I just really like hanging out with my friends. And…I like sleeping.

I really like sleeping because I don't have to think about what the hell I'm going to do with my life after I leave this university. After three years focused on criminal justice, I'm pretty sure it's not for me. What is for me? I don't have a frickin' clue. Yeah – that's what I like about sleeping.

My advisor, Mr. Milton, is a really cool guy. Man, I love that guy. He's dropping hints I should get my master's degree. He recruited me to this school. He wants me to go to some graduate school in Florida. That'd be cool. Palm trees, sunshine – no cold Indiana winter. I could do that. But then what? Be a cop? Work with the juvenile system? FBI? Guard the President?

My favorite thing about sleeping is that I don't have to think about God. Yeah, that's right. I'm tired of thinking about God. I grew up in a Christian home. My parents are over-achievers. My mom teaches in a Christian school and my dad used to be a pastor. Then he became a consultant to churches. He's an insane over-achiever. You wouldn't believe!

He took me on a trip to Africa when I was 12. He taught thousands of pastors. I just hung around. The best thing is that we went hunting in the bush before the conference. I shot a wildebeest. It was awesome. All the "God stuff" was okay – maybe a little over the edge.

Me? I liked youth group. We had a youth pastor – Eric – he was cool. He once caught me smoking a joint. My parents were away on vacation, overseas or somewhere. Some friends came over and brought some weed. I thought I'd try it. Just then, Eric shows up. I thought, "Holy shit! We're busted!"

Eric was really pissed. That hurt. He told my parents when they got home – with me in the room. They were all serious until Eric left. They asked if I learned anything. Like – what are you going to say? I shook my head and looked at my feet. They laughed. They thought it was funny I got busted. My parents cared about me – I felt that. But word got out at youth group. A few people – and a couple of leaders – made fun of me. I felt betrayed – and judged. I thought church was supposed to be about forgiveness. And acceptance. I felt judged. My heart began to drift from church.

Then Eric encouraged me to lead our youth group. I liked that. A few months later, our church got low on money and they shit-canned Eric. I even talked at the meeting. He got screwed. I didn't like church for a long time. I'm not sure I liked God, either.

I started college. I'd go home on weekends. Our family is pretty tight. We have fun. Joke. My parents aren't stuffy-religious. I don't get their commitment. Some things about church frustrate them. But, they're loyal. A little over-the-top-loyal, I think.

In my second year at university, I got into Sig Ep – a fraternity. It's awesome! I love living in community. Most of the guys are on the football team. And, did I mention the parties? We're experts at parties. Our fraternity rocks! It's a family. Total acceptance. No judging. Like church is supposed to be.

During my second year, I didn't go home as much on weekends. The parties went late. I slept in most Saturday and Sunday mornings. I didn't miss church that much, to be honest. When I was home, I just mostly went out of respect to my parents. Church was mostly boring. And the music sucked.

By the third year at school, I became a committed, party-hard fraternity guy, and loved it! I stopped going to church with my parents. I found a community who accepted me for who I was – my fraternity. It was liberating. My parents tolerated it. They encouraged me, but didn't hassle me. I was striking out on my own.

My Sig Ep brothers became my new primary family. Don't get me wrong, I love my family. Even my sister, Laura. She got married to Jason. He's part geek, but he's okay. My new home is with my friends at school. Why not?

My dad tried to weasel me back to church, or God, or…whatever. He tried to get me to go to the Christian Campus House here at Tri-State University. None of my fraternity brothers were part of that. I didn't know anyone there. My parents came to visit and met me at this church near school. I showed up – last minute. Half hung-over. Two, maybe three hours of sleep. I can fake it! I knew what they were up to. I was surprised – one of our football coaches was there. He said, "Hi," but never talked about it at practice.

And God? I don't know. I guess I believe. Or maybe not. Who cares? I mean, besides my parents. Yeah, and probably my sister. But what difference does it make, anyway? I'm scared. I mean, if I was a real Christian, I couldn't really have fun any more. Christians don't have fun, do they? That's what I like about sleeping the most. You don't have to think about stuff. You don't have to think about God. Or life.

I remember my pastor, Paul, always talks about life after death. I can't relate. Hell, I don't even like to think about life after college. You don't have to think about anything when you are sleeping. And, after a few beers, I sleep real good.

Chapter Two
Awake Is a Bad Dream

"Jon, you awake?"

The pounding on the door was a sledge hammer on my head. The autumn sun was streaming in my window. It felt like a warm washcloth on my face. It seemed to say, "Stay right where you are, go back to sleep."

"Jon… you in there?"

I recognized the voice. "Black Jack, is that you?"

"Yeah. Hey, Jon, can I borrow your deodorant?"

Black Jack's always borrowing something. You've got to love him. I could see him before I opened my door. He's standing there in his underwear, just out of the shower. He's a guy who should never wander around in his underwear. The guy's 100% muscle, flab, and hair – all over. Yeah – 350 pounds! He's a lineman everyone would want on his team. I can't imagine playing four quarters against him. You've got to go home bruised.

I'm a defensive end. Second or third string, depending on the coach's mood. I don't play much, but I love the game. I wasn't great in high school, either. I'm not going to be a star, you know what I mean? I probably should have stayed with basketball. But the coach was a jerk. Tried to motivate me by yelling. Pissed me off, and I quit.

My dad cried when I quit basketball. He saw how hard I worked. It was a tense time. He thought I was quitting for the wrong reason. I figured it was none of his business. I still think so.

You shouldn't just quit in a quick decision. That's why I am so stressed. The more I get into criminal justice, the more I don't think it's for me. Problem is, I have no clue what's for me. Why am I on this earth?

I was right. There was Black Jack, standing there all hairy, dressed in his underwear, picking his wedgie. Doesn't matter – we'll be friends forever.

"Hey man, that was an awesome party last night, don't you think?"

"Yeah, I thought it was pretty cool," I said, as my mind wandered to the girls in the corner. "Hey, do you know who those girls were with that redhead? She is really hot."

Black Jack shook his head, "No. I think they were friends of girls from the sorority across the street. Hey, man, thanks for the deodorant. I'll get it back to you later."

"Yeah, that's cool. I'll see you later. You going to Skip's tonight?"

"You want to go?" Black Jack asked as he went down the hall in his underwear.

"Yeah, a bunch of us are meeting over there for a few beers, around nine."

I closed the door, went over to my bed and sat on the edge, looking out the window. The lady in the house next door was taking out the trash. Matt was talking to some guy by his car. My mind wandered to a couple of months back, when I was home for the summer.

"Jon, you all right?" my dad asked. We were in the kitchen. I had just come in for lunch, from the field. We live on a tree farm. I told you my folks were over-achievers. They bought this land just before I was born. It was an old, neglected farm in northeast Indiana. My dad grew up in Michigan. My grandparents had some friends, so the story goes, who had a cabin in the north. They planted trees. My dad got the idea that someday he'd plant some trees.

My parents moved to Indiana because that's the last place my dad was a pastor, before he went full-time into consulting churches. That's when they bought the farm. It was a rundown piece of land, not good for crops. My parents bought it with the idea of planting trees. They got into a government program and ended up planting trees every spring for twenty years, by hand.

I grew up on this farm. When I was in grade school, my dad put me on the big John Deere tractor. I could hardly reach the pedals. My mom was petrified. I didn't really like the work my dad tried to get me to do. I liked spending time with my friends a lot more.

As I got older, my dad introduced me to fishing in our lake and deer hunting in our woods. The trees they planted grew larger. As I grew up, a young forest grew up – all around our house. As I got older, the farm grew on me – it got into my blood. You know what I mean?

On our farm, there were always projects to do. There was always work. As I got older and started lifting weights for football, I could do more. I learned more, too. I learned to service our tractors. I learned how to mow with the big tractor. I learned all about chainsaws. I learned how to prune trees.

During my college years, I had several jobs during the short season between the last day of school in the spring and football camp, which always started the 1st of August. I worked several jobs – Home Depot, Carter Lumber. But, I always worked a second job at the farm. It helped to have spending money.

I had been cleaning a field where they were going to plant 10,000 trees the following spring. That's when I ran into my dad in the kitchen.

"What?" I asked.

"Are you all right?" He asked again. "You're not yourself. You're short to your mother and you just don't seem happy. What's wrong?"

"Nothing," I snapped. It was my usual answer to anything.....and he knew it.

"I think you are not sure about your chosen career," he said.

I was stunned! "How do you know?" I said as I looked him in the eye.

He smiled, even laughed a little. "Well, first of all, I'm your father. Second, I guessed." He continued, "Jon, lots of people study for one thing and end up doing something else. Cut yourself some slack."

I responded, "I'm just not sure about my degree in criminal justice."

His smile disappeared. "Jon, a degree is a degree. You've worked hard for three years. Finish. Finish well. *And then, do whatever.* Most people never ask what your degree was. But they all want to know if you've got a college degree."

It made sense. What bothered me – and what would haunt me – were those words: "and then, do whatever."

In the weeks that followed, I felt lost in the woods with no compass.

Chapter Three
Room For Me

My fraternity brothers were putting together a Saturday afternoon pickup volleyball game in the back yard. I love my third story, corner room. It's the best one in our huge frat house. After my third year at school, I made sure I got back in time to get this room. It faces the east in one corner, so I get the morning sun. It faces the south on the other, which gives me extra warmth in the long, cold, Indiana winter.

In the spring and fall, I can look down on the back yard. This is the spill-over place for parties when the weather's good. It's the place for receptions for parents at the beginning and end of the year. Mr. Milton's not only my faculty advisor, he's also our fraternity advisor. He's really a great guy. How do I tell him I am not sure about criminal justice?

Looking down from my room, I see a lot. No one notices I'm watching. Is that how God is? Does God snoop around and watch people, like ants, screw up their lives? Does God ever do anything, or just watch? The October sun is shining on the bright-colored maple leaves. Then they fall off. Life goes on.

Next year I won't see these leaves, in this back yard, from this room. School will be finished. Another chapter of my life. This won't be my room. Where will I be? What will I do? I've played football for four years in high school and four years in college. Is there life after football? I'm too old to live with my parents. It doesn't feel like home – not to stay – not anymore. It feels like a place to visit. It's not going that well with Sarah. My friends from high school are scattered. My fraternity brothers and friends from this university are going to move all over, following jobs. Some are engaged to get married. Some will go on to graduate school. I can't imagine life after football.

"Here's your deodorant." Black Jack's voice startled me as he came in the door. He could tell I was lost in thought. "You okay?" he asked.

"Yeah, sure," I lied.

How do you tell your friends that, for the first time in your life you don't have a plan? How do you get a plan? How do people find a direction? Is it just dumb luck? Fate? God?

If it's God...? The question stalled in my mind. It seemed – for a moment – the whole world stood still. I looked out the window at the people in the back yard. A couple of my fraternity brothers were firing up the grill and popping a couple of Budweisers. Black Jack was walking out my bedroom door.

"Hey, Black Jack," I said.

"Yeah," he turned around.

"See you tonight at Skip's?"

"Yeah, sure – some of the guys are going to hang out around 9:30?"

"That's cool," I said, as Black Jack disappeared down the hall.

I got to thinking…. The parties are getting a little old. Don't get me wrong, I like hanging out with my friends. It is probably my favorite thing to do. And I like having a few beers – especially with chicken wings. I like the hot sauce…real hot…the best. That, and a cold beer – that's awesome! Yeah, I drink too much. I get drunk…sometimes. Why? Who knows?

Partying, school, and football – that's all we do. Last year, on spring break, I drove my car, full of guys, all the way from northern Indiana to South Padre Island, straight through. Man, that's a long trip. We got a good deal on a place at the beach. It was really cool. That's about all we did: lie out in the sun, party, and drink beer. I can't do this the rest of my life. There must be more. And…football will soon be gone. There must be something for me. How do you find that?

I feel empty.

The Saturday afternoon sun feels so warm in my room. I've got homework to do. It can wait. Screw it. It's only Saturday, I can do it tomorrow.

So here I am, lying on my bed, staring at the ceiling. I've never noticed all the cracks in the paint before. This old house has been around a long time. It used to be a hotel, they say. This is the last year for it. They're going to tear it down and build a new one, next summer. Nothing lasts forever.

I won't last forever. My grandpa died a few years ago. I cried my eyes out. I didn't want to – not around anybody. But I did. I couldn't help it. He was my first relative who died, that I was old enough to know what was going on. He was my mom's dad. He was a gentle man and a strong Christian, too. He and my grandma were always at church. More than that, it was real to him. You could tell. He lived it…walked the talk. You know?. He didn't just go through the motions.

My grandpa's death hit me hard. I think sometimes my friends and I get the idea we're going to live forever. We all know that's bullshit. Everybody dies. Life's short. It seems long – especially during exams. Or when you're 21 points behind in the fourth quarter and the other team's kicking your ass all over the field. But nothing lasts forever. I won't last forever.

I haven't prayed for a long time. I prayed only at church, sort of. I didn't want to offend my parents. But I haven't been to church in a while. And truth is, I don't pray much. I don't get it. I mean, I don't know why people do. Do they think it makes any difference? Hell, I don't even know if I believe God exists.

I stared at the ceiling for a long time. The voices from the back yard drifted from my consciousness. I don't know how it happened. I just started talking to God…or at the ceiling. "God, I don't know what to do with my life. I'm messed up. I don't even know if you're real. I mean, honestly, I don't know if you even exist. If you exist, show me. And give me some kind of direction. I've got no clue."

The sun was still warm. I must have fallen asleep. I like to sleep. You don't have to think. I think I dreamed about high school…a less complicated time.

Chapter Four
A Short Summer

It was just after graduation from high school. I had an awesome senior year. I never did become a star at football. I like the "family feel" of the team. It's like a community! Coach awarded me the mental attitude award. I remember my parents thinking it was a big deal. The coach said, in front of the whole auditorium, it was the best award, because there is "life after football." Whatever.

I applied to Tri-State University and got accepted. My grades weren't the best in high school – but good enough to get in. During my senior year, I met Mr. Milton. He was teaching a criminal justice class at the police station in Kendallville. It was only for seniors. We got "release time" for a whole afternoon, a couple of days each week, to go to this class. It counted for college credit, too. A girl in my class talked me into it. I liked getting out of school for "release time." It's the main reason I went.

Mr. Milton took a liking to me right away. It wasn't like there was a lot of competition. Most of the kids who took that class weren't bound for college. They were headed for the police academy. But not me. College was always my option.

My parents have a lot of education. My mom has a master's degree. She's a teacher in a preschool. My dad has two doctorates. He jokes about it – says he's a slow learner. He does have ADD. That's where both my sister, Laura, and I got it – from him. Laura has her master's degree in special education. Yeah, college, from the beginning, has been on my family's agenda.

I don't know if Mr. Milton had some influence with my acceptance to Tri-State or not. When I met him, he was an attorney who taught high school kids on the side. Later, I learned, he had a job offer to teach criminal justice at Tri-State. Anyway, I got accepted.

I really wanted to go to Ball State University in Muncie, Indiana. Some of my friends went there. I thought we could really party. My parents thought that, too. They figured I needed more structure. They met Mr. Milton, and he told them he would be my advisor. Tri-State was more expensive, but they wanted to make sure I finished. They thought Mr. Milton would help me through.

The best part for me was that Tri-State had a football team. Being a smaller school, I had a chance to make the team. Ball State was huge. The competition would probably leave me behind. It seemed like a good choice. It was closer to home. I wasn't sure how it would feel being further away.

Besides, I knew the Tri-State campus. During my high school basketball days, I went to Tri-State basketball camp every summer. One year, I went to three camps in a row! I wonder where I picked up that over-achiever mentality?

It was great to graduate. I liked DeKalb High School in a lot of ways. It was a good school for me. I made a lot of really good friends there. Nick, Nate, Mackenzie, Tommy – dozens more, even a few girls. Yeah – these will be my best friends forever. Yeah, these relationships. That's what life's all about. But I'm ready to move on.

I got a job at Home Depot and I'm working on my parent's farm. At Home Depot, I stock shelves and help customers. I'm learning about construction. I like being involved with people, and the variety of jobs. It doesn't get boring. I go to the gym and lift weights every day. On the farm, I'm helping in a lot of ways, too. The farm is a great place. I shot my first deer when I was 9. I've gotten several since.

I'm a little nervous about going to college. But I'm excited about playing football. I'm reporting to football camp on August 1, so it'll be a short, busy summer. I'll earn as much money as I can. I'm ready for that.

My dad left after my graduation on another trip. He travels a lot, helping churches. He's called the "Church Doctor." He knows a lot about all kinds of churches, and goes all over the world. He's written several books. I have them all, but I've never read any of them. I don't like to read. I read just what I have to, to get by in school.

My dad's in England right now. Some friend of his – a pastor named Walt from a huge church in Phoenix – suggested he go and check out what's happening with Christianity there. It's supposed to be a big deal. Attracting a lot of young adults. If it is, I'm guessing they don't have much to do. Maybe they're so bored they go to church. My dad took four pastors with him. A medical doctor friend of his helped pay his way. Imagine that! This doctor operated on my dad's sinuses a few years ago. It turns out he's a Christian who's excited about missions – reaching new people. So he helps my dad, financially.

My dad raises his own salary. What's up with that? He works way too hard, in my opinion. His Board of Directors sets his salary and then he has to find people who will support our family. He's been doing this for years – before I was born. It's weird. It seems like begging. I can't believe people do it. Maybe they're just rich and can't figure out what to do with their spare money. I don't have that problem. That's why I'm working my butt off.

I am really liking my two jobs, though. I like seeing some money in my bank account. I need to buy some clothes. My mom's off for the summer from teaching. She's very supportive. She does all the shopping in our house – except for farm stuff. She's a good cook and you can tell she loves me and my sister.

My sister's in her last year of college, starting this fall. This summer she's working at Bob Evans. She's a hard worker,. We go there and eat. We take my grandparents. I've never eaten so often at Bob Evans before. My parents and grandparents give her huge tips – about as much as the meal costs. They're generous people.

"What you doing, Jon?" my mom asked as she came into the kitchen.

"I'm making a sandwich. I'm taking a little break before I go out and mow the field across the pond."

"Your dad's coming home from England tomorrow night. Think you'd like to go along and pick him up at the airport?" she asked.

"Yeah, sure," I said. "Maybe we could stop and get a burger after we pick him up?"

I'm always hungry. I could never guess what my dad would report about what happened in England. I couldn't imagine how it would reorganize my whole life four years later.

Chapter Five
A Short Window

My dad arrived at the Fort Wayne Airport about 9:30 p.m. I spotted him coming down the escalator. He looked tired, but he had a smile of enthusiasm. "It must have been a good trip," I thought. I had no idea!

I was in England quite a few years earlier, when I was 12. It was after the mission trip in Africa and the wildebeest hunt. We flew to London from Johannesburg. My mom and Laura met us at Heathrow Airport in London. They used my dad's gazillion frequent flier miles. We spent a week in England before traveling throughout the continent of Europe. We visited Bath and Stonehenge while we were in England, too. I remember, at Stonehenge, my dad just sat on a bench forever trying to contemplate what it could be all about. It must be his consultant's curiosity. I thought we would never leave!

My favorite part of England was the original Hard Rock Café. Some man served us, wearing a dress. My sister and I had done some homework about England. Well, most of it was Laura. She found out that London is where they built the very first Hard Rock Café. She also found out, somehow, that kids can drink one beer, when they are with their parents, at a restaurant or pub. So when we got to the Hard Rock Café, we ordered burgers and Laura and I ordered a beer. My parents were shocked! They said, "You can't do that." Then they looked at the man in the dress, "They can't do that...can they?" Yeah, we got the beers. We found out neither of us liked beer – at least at that age.

"How was England?" I asked my dad.

"It was unbelievable," he said.

I thought he was in London, but he wasn't. He was in the north. A place called Sheffield. "I never heard of it," I said.

"Neither had I," he explained. "My friend, Walt, was the one who insisted that, with my work helping churches, I had to see what was going on there."

"So, what was it like?" my mom asked, as we got in the car to leave the airport.

"You wouldn't believe it," Dad said, with more excitement than any person should have after a long trip. "You know, I've been all over the world – Asia, South America, Africa, Europe, India, Philippines, and the former Soviet Union. I've seen some exciting places where God is really changing lives. But I have never seen anything like this. It blew me away, the way God is impacting the lives of the people through this movement."

"What's the name of the church?" my mom asked. She can't keep track of all the places he goes, either.

"It's St. Thomas' Anglican/Baptist Church," he said. "I know it's kind of weird. It's a combination of an Anglican church – as in the Church of England – and a Baptist church. And, they gather in two different locations, in two different parts of the city. But both are Anglican/Baptist churches."

"What makes it so special?" my mom asked. She'd heard my dad's excitement about churches before.

He tried to explain. "It's the culture. They have the closest thing to the culture of the New Testament Church I've ever seen anywhere. It's part of their DNA. They behave like the people of the Bible, in the early church – more than I have ever seen."

I joked, "I knew you were old, Dad! You knew people in Bible?"

"Funny, Jon," he said. "No. But if you look at how the church grew – changed the world, impacted the Roman Empire. The way these early Christians lived. Their behavior was driven by their culture: their values, beliefs, priorities, attitudes, and worldviews. That culture is what we help churches get back to. It's what really changes churches for good. The modern church has drifted so far…."

My attention span ran out at that point. My dad is the master of TMI – too much information! He had moved to lecture mode. He gets too excited about God stuff. But then he got my attention in a way that had never, ever, happened before.

"Something else happened while I was there. I stayed with Mick, one of the pastors, and his wife. One day Mick and I were having breakfast at his house and we were talking about…I don't even know what!" My dad paused trying to find the words. "I heard God speak to me. It was clear, and audible."

I'd never heard my dad talk like that before!

He continued, "The voice…God said, 'You should bring groups from North America here. This is a movement. It is as much caught as taught. They are like vessels. They can carry this movement back to North America.'"

I thought, "That's cool, now my dad's hearing voices. I wonder what he had for breakfast." I was skeptical and totally unprepared for what he said next.

"Simultaneous to that," he said, "I got another, totally unexpected message. God said, 'You are supposed to bring your son here – soon, and Pastor Bob.'"

At this point, I was thinking my dad totally lost it. It is one thing if God wants to talk to him, or if he thinks God is talking to him. But what does that have to do with me? And what's the deal with Pastor Bob from our church? What's up with that?

I just thought to myself, this is a long way from normal. People don't just "hear from God." My dad then said he had never had that happen before. It seemed so strange, even to him.

Before I could ask, my dad explained, "I didn't know what to think. So I told Mick: 'I think God just spoke to me.'"

Dad said he was uncomfortable sharing that with Mick, since they did not know each other very well.

"So, what did Mick say?" my mom asked.

"He said, 'If God told you, then you better do it,'" my dad said. "But, I said, 'Why? Why would God want me to do that?' Mick just said, 'You don't always know why. Sometimes that's not your job. Just be faithful to what God says.' So, I'm telling you. And tomorrow I'll talk with Pastor Bob."

Personally, I wondered what planet this guy Mick was from. What kind of church was this? I figured it would never happen. The money had to be raised. As for me, it was just a few weeks before I was off to football camp. My dad understood the skepticism and used the old line, "If God is in it, it'll happen."

A week later, Dad had a luncheon appointment with his medical doctor friend. He was going to thank him for sponsoring his trip and report about it. It was a Tuesday, my day off at Home Depot. I was working on the farm and had just come in for lunch. We met in the kitchen. Seeing me, Dad got a last-minute idea and invited me to go along to lunch. I never turn down a free lunch.

At Applebee's, Dad introduced me to Dr. Bill. My dad told the story of all he saw in Sheffield. He even told him the God-talking story. He told him he had a short window of time to take me to England. In addition, he told Dr. Bill that Pastor Bob would like to take his daughter, Alicia. I was surprised the doctor didn't think my dad was a lunatic. Instead, he reached into his suit coat pocket, pulled out a checkbook and wrote a check for $5,000: for Dad, me, Pastor Bob, and Alicia to go to England! I couldn't believe it.

Chapter Six
A Word Is Planted

There I was, a few weeks before I reported to football camp, on my way to England for…God-only-knows-what. I figured, I get to quit work a couple of weeks early, take a trip to a part of England I've never seen – all at the expense of Dr. Bill, who I spent a total of 45 minutes with at lunch. Why not?

We arrived in Manchester, England, and took the train across to Sheffield. There I met Mick, and his wife and daughter. Alicia and I stayed at the house of a young couple from the church. Pastor Bob stayed with someone else and my dad stayed, again, with Mick and his family. The young couple took Alicia and me all over Sheffield. It's a good sized city, with several universities, typical narrow British streets, a large number of clubs that attract university students, and, of course, thousands of pubs!

I really liked the people we met. I've never seen people my age so excited to be Christians. They seemed genuine, too. They were not religious fanatics, or weird. They seemed like normal people, but there was something very different about them. They had it together, you know what I mean?

They have challenges in life like everybody, but they seem to have purpose, direction. They actually like going to church – it didn't even seem like a duty.

I met some university students who were from around England. They had found summer jobs in Sheffield. Even though their parents were far away, they were involved in this church – and wanted to be. That seemed strange to me, for some reason.

My dad is always trying to help churches reach out to people who aren't Christians. But, these people seem to do it because they actually like to. It seems part of their life. They also have a good time doing it.

My youth pastor, Eric, was a bit like that. I thought he was enthusiastic because it was his job – you know, he had to put on a good act in front of the kids like me at the church. Yet, he seemed genuine enough. I never met anyone else like that. The last thing I expected was to find others like him in England.

We got to visit the countryside, what they call the Peak District. It's beautiful. Large rolling hills, reservoirs, forests, and English villages with old churches and little shops. We even got to see Little John's grave – you know, the guy who hung out with Robin Hood? We also got into some pubs and had some great meals. Pubs are not like bars in the U.S. They're more family-friendly. They're places where you watch sports, talk to your neighbors, and strangers become friends. It's all about relationships. I like that. Pubs are neighborhood gathering places – community halls with food and beer. They don't feel like commercial destinations. They're more a part of life.

Somewhere in this whirlwind introduction to Sheffield and St. Thomas' Church, I met a few young adults who are involved in what they call FORM. I had no idea what this would mean for my life four years later.

It's funny. Sometimes you do something, or meet someone, and it just seems like another everyday occurrence – nothing special. I mean no bells or whistles go off, the earth doesn't shake, no lightning. It's just like another day of life, another person you meet, another place you visit. Something you'll maybe forget. You might take some pictures, and look at them once or twice, maybe post them on Facebook. Someday you throw them away. They are just more clutter in your journey.

Then there are these…I don't know…"God moments." They seem just so ordinary, nothing special. You have no clue then – and maybe for a long time in the future. At the time, you're not even aware. You're not ready. The dots are not connected. You don't even see the dots. That's because you're not looking. I wasn't looking.

My eyes were on football, criminal justice, a fraternity. It was just days from my university adventure. I had no idea that the embryo of my greatest journey was birthed as I met these students in FORM. No idea at all.

FORM is a 10-month training program for young adults. At Mick's church, it's for those just out of university – a year off before the job market. My first thought, when I met Ben and Andy, was why, after four years of university, would anyone want to go through another year of school – especially a religious school?

"It's not like that," said Ben, "…not at all. It's the most fun I've ever had."

Andy added, "You go to the university as an investment in your career. But you take ten months of FORM to let God invest in you, as a person. That changes everything."

"Yeah," continued Ben, "It's a discipleship year. You learn more about who God really is. You also learn who He has made you to uniquely be. You learn about yourself."

"Don't you think everyone already gets that?" I asked politely.

"Not at all!" said Ben. "Most people only think they know who they are. They learn all this stuff at university, but they never asked God to teach them about themselves. Besides, we do hands-on ministry. We get involved in helping the poor, working with children, interacting with other cultures, connecting with university students. Most people go through life and never get those experiences. Yeah, and we have a lot of fun along the way. We live together in community: guys are in two houses and the girls share a couple of houses. We become family. We go on mission excursions around the country and take a trip outside of the country together. It is a once-in-a-lifetime opportunity to do FORM."

I have to admit, I was momentarily intrigued. When Alicia and I saw my dad and Pastor Bob at Mick's house a couple of days later, I made an announcement: "I know we're supposed to go back home tomorrow, but I have a few days before football camp. Alicia and I have decided to stay here in England and hang out with these people. We'll come home later, okay?"

I saw my dad look at Pastor Bob, who looked at him. Then they looked at Mick, who looked at each of them, and then they looked at each other again. It was a long silence, like everybody just discovered a pink elephant in the room. I think the pink elephant was me and it just took a dump! I could tell the idea wasn't going to fly.

My dad broke the silence, "That won't work. It would cost a fortune to change your tickets. Besides, you might not get on another plane. Planes are really booked going overseas. Besides, you need to finish the work on the farm, pack, and move to school."

The comment broke the dream into pieces of reality. I knew he was right. I felt a little foolish. Mick added, "You'll be back someday."

As we said goodbye, Mick prayed over us. He paused, put his hands on my shoulders, and said, "I have a word from God for you, Jon. I sense God is saying that you are a mighty warrior for God."

I was speechless.

Chapter Seven
University: S.W.A.T. or What?

On the train from Sheffield to Manchester Airport, I could tell my dad was having some kind of religious buzz about this "word from God" about me being a "mighty warrior for God." He even asked me what I thought about it.

"Yeah, what was that all about?" I asked. It seemed a bit strange to me and really irrelevant. I would have gone for something like, "God has big plans for you in football. You will be recruited on a scholarship to a Division 1 school. You will be drafted in the second round of the NFL draft." Ok, maybe that would be a little unrealistic. But a "mighty warrior for God" was not even on my radar screen...yet.

My car was packed full of stuff for school. I moved into the freshman dorm the night before football camp began on August 1. "My life is changing, a new chapter of history," I thought to myself. It was scary, but I felt a sense of personal graduation. Not just beyond high school, but life on my own – out of my parents' house. All of a sudden it became real: "I actually made it to college." That was my happy thought. On the reality side was uncertainty, "Can I make it through?"

"Hi, my name is Jon. I'm your roommate," I said as I carried my first box into my first home away from home.

"Hey, I'm Greg," he replied. We shook hands and he introduced his parents who had just finished helping him move in.

"You on the football team?" I asked. He had to be. No one comes to school a month early. "What position do you play?" I asked.

Greg responded, "I'm an offensive guard."

We talked about where we were from, and a little about our high schools. That was our transition conversation to a new world.

About four weeks after school started, I learned about Greg's priorities. His first priority was Melinda, his girlfriend from high school who also came to Tri-State. His second priority was football. A distant third was getting an education.

Greg's and my relationship began with tension about the fifth week into the new semester. He asked me to move out so Melinda could sleep in. I didn't want to rat on him. There's a certain code of loyalty on football teams, and he was taking full advantage of it...and me. I ended up sleeping on a couch in another room of football players.

But my computer and desk were in my room. It was an awkward scene, and it started to affect my grades.

I was home one weekend and told my parents. They reacted more strongly than I thought. They said, "We're paying for your room so you can get an education, not so Greg can have sex." I went to my advisor, Mr. Milton. He said I had to confront Greg, myself, first. Then I could get help from the dorm leader, if that didn't work. I didn't want to do it, but I did.

As it turned out, Greg was failing his classes. He and his girlfriend left school. There were others who also dropped out along the way. It was harder than I thought. So was football. But I loved it! I began thinking about joining a fraternity the next year. And I did!

The first two years of college were mostly general classes. My major focused on criminal justice but I also took a lot of extra psychology classes – almost enough for a double major. I got a part-time job working for a social agency. They called it supervised visitation for fathers or mothers who wanted to visit their kids. They were divorced or separated. Most had criminal records and were not allowed to be alone with their children unless supervised. I was a supervisor. One parent would drop off the kids at the agency and would leave. Then the other would arrive and would spend time with the kids while I watched. It was an interesting experience. I learned a lot.

For a while, in the wide range of choices of criminal justice, I thought it would be cool to be part of the S.W.A.T. team. Then I met someone who strongly encouraged me not to do that. She claimed it wrecked their marriage for her husband to be in that stressful world. It changed my mind. My mom was glad – she was worried about my safety.

Then I thought I'd go into the juvenile part of criminal justice. But the more I got into it, the more uncertain I became. Toward the end of my second year, I began to focus on more criminal justice courses. Some were better than others. We had a few field trips and some hands-on demonstrations. When we learned about tasers, I volunteered to be tased. I wouldn't recommend it!

Meanwhile, the partying continued. The beer flowed. I had great times with my friends. I worked really hard at my schoolwork– especially certain courses. Some were harder than others. I got fairly good grades.

By the beginning of my fourth year, I was sure of several things: I wanted to finish school and get the degree. And I would work to finish well. I would try not to get hung up about my future career. I would try not to beat myself up because of my doubts that criminal justice – at least that was the theory.

In practice, I felt like I was in crisis mode. I didn't know what I was going to do. Other students were already having job interviews. That's when I prayed and asked God to show me that He was real. I laid on my bed, stared at the ceiling. I asked God to give me some direction.

Then I fell back asleep, the warm summer sun bathing me in friendliness. I became oblivious to the growing party in the back yard. I didn't wake up until 4:30 that afternoon. It was time to take a shower and clean up. The party is beginning to take off, and I need to grab some dinner. The guys are going to meet at Skip's at 9:30 p.m. The night is young! I'm unsettled. But I'll push on. I'll get through school. Even if I don't know…for what.

Chapter Eight
Does God E-mail?

The week at school was hard. About every course had tests or papers due. On Saturday morning, our football team lost a tight battle with a school from Wisconsin. It was a home game, too. My parents were there. They're just about always there. I played only a few minutes. My parents don't seem to care. They love football. They love me. I hope I can be a parent like that.

We went out for lunch after the football game. My parents like to treat me to a nice meal. I tried to be positive about my struggle. I didn't say anything about my anxiety – not knowing what to do with my life. Actually, I was so busy with school and football I didn't have much time or energy to think about it.

My parents didn't ask me about church the next day. I appreciated the space. I didn't need the hassle. But I thought about going. I wondered, since I asked God for direction, should I go to church? I was bargaining with God. It seemed logical, sort of a divine/human form of "you scratch my back, I'll scratch yours."

My parents left and I went to a party that night. It was a great party at the sorority down the street. They always have good parties. I got in about 3:30 a.m. I didn't go to church the next day. I didn't even think about it.

On Thursday, I got an e-mail. It wasn't just any e-mail. It wasn't from my parents, or sister and brother-in-law, or any friend from high school or around Tri-State. It was from Mick – the pastor in England. You know, the one who had the "word from the Lord," the one who said, "You will be a mighty warrior for God." I couldn't believe it! It was three and a half years ago that I was in England with my dad, Pastor Bob, and Alicia.

At first, I couldn't believe Mick even remembered who I was. Then, I thought about my dad. He takes groups over there every June for about a week. It was then I wondered if my dad and Mick had talked and planned the e-mail.

Mick didn't say anything about my dad. He challenged me to pray and ask God if He would direct me to apply to take FORM, in England, the following September – for 10 months. This was a few days after I prayed to God to show me if He was real, to give me a sign. To provide for me a direction. Was that spooky, or what? I told no one about my prayer – not even my parents. No one! Could this be a coincidence? What should I do?

I called home that Thursday night. My dad was in town and both of my parents were on the phone. I told them I got an e-mail from Mick. My dad was surprised.

"Really," he said, "from Mick? What for? What did he say?"

"He wants me to think about applying to take FORM next September in England," I said.

"Really?" my mom returned.

My dad added, "You know, every year I take that group to England. I stay with Mick and his family. He always asks about our family, and every year he asks where you are in school – what year. This last June I told him you were entering your last year. But that was the end of the conversation. He never said another word. I thought he was just being polite. He asked about mom, Laura, and Jason, too. He always does – but that's all he says. I always ask about his family, too."

My parents were totally surprised. I was shocked. Mick suggested I go to the website and check it out. Now, suddenly, I had a whole new set of issues to think about.

My dad said, "Just pray about it. Do what God leads you to do."

Normally, I would have said something like, "How does that work?" But, unknown to my parents, or anyone, I had just prayed several days earlier – and then this – right out of nowhere…or, maybe not!

What do you do when a God-event occurs? I had no practice at this sort of thing. I didn't want to go to my parents – "they want me to do anything that's Christian" – I thought. I did decide to pray about it. It seems odd, because I had no other ideas about what to do with my life. But maybe something else would come up.

It was a lot to think about. How do you know if you are doing what God wants? Or is there anything God really wants you to do or not do? I mean, besides not killing someone or stealing – all that stuff in the Ten Commandments. What about normal stuff? Does God even care what you do? And, if God cares, how do you know? Even if FORM was a great thing to do, how do I know it's a good thing for me? And how do I know it's the right time for me to do it now, and not some other time? After the phone call with my parents, I fell asleep thinking about all this.

Going to England for a couple of weeks, seeing the wax museum, riding the London Eye Ferris Wheel, seeing the Big Ben clock, visiting Westminster Abbey, that's one thing. It's a different thing to go to Sheffield (where all that good stuff isn't) and stay there for 10 months! That's just about a whole year! No going home for the weekend!

If that's not enough, I thought about the religious part of it. Am I ready for that? I remembered – three and a half years ago – talking to Andy and Ben, who took FORM. They were on the streets praying with homeless people and loved it! That scares the crap out of me. I didn't know if I was ready for that. Who is? Would I ever be? You can't go try it out for a week – it's a 10-month deal. When I was there, I was with my dad, Alicia, and Pastor Bob. No one I know would be there except for the few people I met. I am guessing they go to church every Sunday. I haven't done that for years. My mind was racing.

Chapter Nine
Life at the Crossroads

I looked at the FORM website and put the idea in the back of my mind – for months. I focused on football. But, at the end of the season, I started thinking about it again. What would I do next year?

It's a big decision to take 10 months out of your life. If you live to be 70, that's 1 percent of your life. On the other hand, look how much time you spend preparing to make a living. When I saw Andy and Ben, and other young adults, they were talking about an experience where they invested 10 months, not to make a living, but to discover life.

My mind was rambling with these questions as I made my way to see Mr. Milton. He wanted me to go to grad school in Florida. Maybe he would talk me out of it. We spend so much time filling our heads. We focus so much effort on filling our stomachs. What do we put into filling our hearts, our character, who we are, and all we can become? Heck, that's too philosophical. But, deep down, I was really wondering: who am I? What is my purpose in life? Where is life – for me?

One of the reasons Criminal Justice seemed so attractive was that I wanted to make a difference. This world is full of bad people who do terrible things. They deserve justice. Those who are called to that career really help. But they're dealing with the symptoms.

I got to thinking about a sermon my dad preached when he filled in one Sunday last summer for Pastor Paul. He said, "We can't police everyone, all the time. What if we could influence a lot of people not to live selfishly, hurt, rob, be unfaithful, and all that stuff? What if people knew God's love that goes beyond justice? Justice is when you get what you deserve. Mercy is when you don't get what you deserve. Grace is when you get what you don't deserve." Yeah, I know a little bit about Christianity – I just didn't know how to live it, or deliver it to others. Then again, I don't know. I thought that maybe I just ought to go to grad school for criminal justice.

"Hi, Jon, it's good to see you," Mr. Milton greeted me at the office door. "How have you been?"

"Good," I replied, stretching the truth, with a positive spin.

"How's football?" he asked.

"Oh, it's going okay. I hate to see four years come to an end. Eight years if you count high school. It'll be different," I shared more honestly.

"And the grades…from my reports, you are off to a pretty good start this year. How do you feel about it?" he asked.

"Not too bad. I think I finally figured out how to study," I answered.

"So what can I do for you today, Jon?" asked Mr. Milton.

"Well, I am just wondering. You talked to me last spring about grad school. You mentioned Florida Gulf Coast University. My dad had a consultation in the Orlando area a while ago, and I took a couple of days and went with him. We rented a car, after he was finished, and drove down toward Fort Myers. We made an appointment with the

dean of the grad school and he set up a couple of appointments with professors. That's a really cool place – lakes, beaches, palm trees, an awesome athletic facility, and aquatic center. It looks like a resort."

He interrupted, "Yes, but you still have to work – grad school isn't a vacation – even there."

"Yeah, I know," I returned. "The thing is, I have this opportunity to study at this church in England for 10 months. It is a discipleship training program. Anyway, I told the dean in Florida about it and asked for his ideas of what I should do. He surprised me by saying he spent a year in Germany – one of the best experiences of his life. He said if I had a chance to spend time in England, I should do that first. Then, if I am still interested in pursuing criminal justice, come back and see him."

Mr. Milton added, "I know him, he's a good man."

I continued, "When I left his office, I told my dad, 'That guy is more interested in me than getting more students.' My dad said, 'If he's interested in students first, he'll build a great grad school.'"

Mr. Milton paused and pondered for a moment, "Jon, I just think this opportunity in England would be perfect for you at this time. You're not tied down with a marriage or a home. I think you should consider it."

I couldn't believe it. I thought most people were selfish and all they wanted was business for their schools. But this was a really quality guy. My admiration for him went even higher – and it was already, I thought, about as high as it could be.

I started to look further into FORM. I learned later that my parents were praying hard: that I would make the right decision for me, and hoping it might be to apply to FORM. My dad told me later that he had been to Sheffield several times. Each year, there was a different group of students in the FORM training. In June of every year, when my dad goes there, the FORM group that year is just completing the experience. He says he's never seen young adults so on fire for God, and yet, they are sensible, mature, and trained so well. My dad says he's not seen anything like it anywhere. He says that once they're trained, they are valuable assets to churches. He thinks that if enough of these young adults are trained, it could change our world. But you know...that's my dad.

I looked, again, at the website. I learned that they do a lot of fun things together. They all have regular jobs, part-time. They work on Mondays, Wednesdays, and Fridays. That helps with expenses and pays the rent. They have teaching when they come together on Tuesdays and Thursdays. All the teachers are uniquely selected. They're volunteers and they teach on what they're really excited about and where they have experience. Then, on weekends, they have time for worship and mission excursions, where they go out and spend a weekend somewhere. They also have parties – lots of parties. Then, in the spring, they take an overseas mission trip.

My first impression is that this is like a Christian fraternity, a community, a family – with both men and women. That sounds like fun!

I filled out the application. The next step was a Skype interview with the leaders. It was a friendly conversation. Their names were Dan and Jude and they were very excited about the upcoming year. I started to get a little excited, too.

When I heard I was accepted, it was a great relief. By then, I really wanted to do it. But now, reality set in. I got a little nervous. Will I fit? Can I do this? Are they all super-religious types? Can you drink a beer once in a while? These questions just kept coming.

But I had a school year to finish: exams to take, papers to write, reports to complete. I at least knew– sort of – what I would be doing next year.

Chapter Ten
The End of the Beginning

Graduation from Tri-State University was a great milestone for me. It's a confidence booster when you accomplish something, isn't it? My parents and grandparents were there. So was my sister and brother-in-law. I am sure my parents were glad to see their second – and last – child get through college. Did I mention tuition bills stopped for them?

I thought about some of my favorite high school friends: Nate, Nick, and Mackenzie. I miss seeing them. I love these guys like brothers. We will always be close friends. You know – they really are great guys. Their parents are good parents – really good. They're nice people, supportive and encouraging. Oh yeah, my friends get sideways with their parents once in a while, but who doesn't?

How did I ever make it through college? I don't pretend to know this stuff, but part of it, I really think, is that I had a serious support mechanism in Mr. Milton. He was like a parent, except at school – for the school, about the school. Believe it or not, I think a second part of it was football. I had a goal: to play four years. When you are in football, at

Tri-State, you have to keep your grades up. You're part of a study table. You are watched closely on your grades. The minute you start slipping, the coaches know. Your advisor knows. And help is on the way. I think I needed that structure. That's one of the things my parents liked about Tri-State. That's probably part of the reason it costs more. My parents didn't make me go here. But, I am glad I listened to their encouragement.

Another reason that made a difference: I had another goal. Yeah, one goal was to play football. But at first, it was to study criminal justice. I really thought that was for me. That helped me through the first three years. Then, I hit the wall, and had no goal. Then, the goal was to "finish well" – as my dad said – and get the degree. I guess it's okay if your goals change from time to time. They get you through. I think it's bad when you don't have a goal. It's also good to have support mechanisms. At least it works for me.

After the graduation ceremony, our fraternity had a picnic lunch in the back yard. There was Mr. Milton and his wife grilling burgers and hotdogs, mixing with the parents. I am going to stay connected with Mr. Milton. He's way more than an advisor. He's a friend.

After the party, my dad told me he had a nice talk with Mr. Milton. Dad said he was a little nervous because he knew Mr. Milton was the one who influenced me to go into criminal justice. My dad wondered if he might be disappointed about me going to England and doing FORM.

But Mr. Milton told my dad that England was the right thing for me.

I wonder why Mr. Milton is so supportive about England and FORM. I don't know if he's a Christian or even religious. I would like to know. I just don't have the guts to ask him. My dad was glad to hear about his support. He knew Mr. Milton carries a lot of weight with me.

My parents hung around for a long time at the party. I was busy saying good bye to all my fraternity buddies. It was hard to believe I might never see some of these guys again. We've become like family. It's hard to move on. When I finally sat down with my parents, my mom talked about my next chapter of life in England. She said it seemed like such an unlikely next step.

"A year ago, I could never have guessed it was possible you would live overseas," Mom said. I think she was already wondering how much she would miss me. I began to think the same thing about my parents, Laura and Jason, my friends, the Indianapolis Colts, Buffalo Wild Wings – you know, all the stuff you take for granted.

The summer went by so fast! My parents bought an adjacent farm and were clearing the land to plant more trees. Now they were connected with a program from the U.S. Fish and Wildlife Service. They got our whole tree farm certified as a wildlife habitat. The added land had fields, woods, and two lakes. I spent the summer clearing the field of brush, small trees, and junk. It would get planted with 9,000 hardwood trees the next spring. I liked the outdoor work. And, I'm beginning to understand my parents' dreams for the future of our farm.

Before I was born, my mom and dad started planting trees for one week, each spring. It was during spring break, when my mom was off school. My dad would take a vacation week. The state nursery would supply the trees at cost: thousands of them every year.

My parents are either really smart, or really crazy, depending on how you look at it. The day they planted the first tree, they knew they'd never live to see income from the timber. Trees take too long to grow! But they put the whole farm in a trust. When my parents are gone, my sister, Laura, and I are going to be trustees. The trust directs the money from the sale of the trees to go to mission work.

Laura and I, and our spouses – if we are married (I'm not but Laura is), will make decisions on where the money will go. The timber has been planted over several decades and will continue to be planted. So the timber harvests will continue over several decades, in the future.

I think my parents know a lot about missions that struggle from a lack of resources. My dad has operated Church Doctor Ministries as a nonprofit for more than 30 years. They help anyone who needs it – and give away materials to help pastors all over the world. They are always on the edge of broke. Yeah, I think they want to help other mission groups to accomplish more, without the stress.

So, I'm clearing this field. But I am beginning to catch on, that I'm helping to invest in the future. There are those who live in debt. They are behind. There are those who live paycheck to paycheck. They are current. Then, there are a few who invest in the future.

Maybe that's what this FORM thing is all about. Maybe I'm investing in my future. It's kind of strange. I had a plan: criminal justice and football. Then I had no plan. Then I got that e-mail from Mick. So now, I have a plan. What does it mean? I have no idea. What am I getting myself into? I have no clue. My dad says it's a "leap of faith." Have you ever taken a leap like that?

Chapter Eleven
Across the Pond

"So how do you feel about going?" Nick asked.

Nick is probably my closest friend from high school. He was a defensive back in high school, I was a wide receiver. We were always together. We had a lot of good times. During our college years, we would go a few months without seeing each other. He moved to Ball State University in Muncie, Indiana, about two hours away from our homes. I went north to Angola, the home of Tri-State University, now called Trine University. Funny, I graduated from Tri-State, and as soon as I did, they changed the name. Does that mean I graduated from a school that no longer exists? Just shows you how the world is continuing to change. Nothing lasts forever.

"So, what do you think?" Nick asked again.

"Sorry," I said, "my mind was wandering."

"You've got, what, nine days left?" Nick tried again.

"You make it sound like I'm dying, Nick. I'm just going for 10 months to England."

When close friends separate for a time, I guess it is a little like dying. Except, I hope, I come back. I wasn't really scared. I had traveled with my parents a lot. I remember once, my dad had frequent flier miles that were going to expire on United Airlines. He put a route map on the table and said to Laura and me, "We're going somewhere on spring break. We have enough frequent flier miles for all of us to go for free, anywhere United flies. Pick a place – anywhere in the world."

We picked Bangkok, Thailand! That's a long way to go for spring break. My mom was hoping to go to Hawaii…. But we heard Dad talk about his several trips to Thailand. He loves it there. So we spent a week south of Bangkok, on the beach, in the Gulf of Siam.

But my friend, Nick, has never been out of the U.S. He didn't even have a passport. My dad calls this a worldview issue. People have different worldviews based on their experiences, like travel. That dean at Florida Gulf Coast University – the one who spent a year after college in Germany – I think he knew living in another country would expand my worldview.

My parents did that their second year of marriage. My dad was at seminary in St. Louis, Missouri. He took a second year of seminary in Australia. They lived there for 14 months. They talk about it a lot. So I expected that living in England would expand my worldview.

Little did I realize how FORM would change my worldview. Everything you learn messes with your worldview – for good, or for bad. Studying criminal justice changed my worldview. Heck, volunteering for the taser changed my worldview! Let me tell you, if you see a cop coming with a taser, do whatever he says. Trust me!

As I finished my packing, my dad told me, again, about the students he met from FORM during all his trips to Sheffield, England. He smiled and said, "You'll never be the same."

I figured he was exaggerating a little. He said he had never met young adults so confident in a wholesome way. I am not sure what that means, but it sounds good. He said they really get Christianity at a level most people don't. He said they are content, happy, excited people. He said they know how to live the faith, and impact others for good – more than he did after he finished four years of seminary. It seems hard to believe. Maybe he forgets.

The day arrived: it was time to go. It was a day of...feelings. You know what I mean? I was excited and nervous. I was confident and had doubts. I felt the same way the first day of high school, the first day of football practice, the first day of college. Maybe everybody does.

This was a little more intense. Further away. More than a vacation. And whatever this FORM is really all about.

All these feelings were joined between two major convictions. First, I was not quitting, no matter how ugly it got. Second, my dad arranged my ticket for a return for Christmas, so I knew I'd see everyone at home in less than four months. I can stand anything for four months, no matter how bad it gets.

My parents took me to the airport in Fort Wayne. Laura and Jason were at the airport, and so were my grandparents, on my dad's side. I hugged everyone. We are a close family. Everyone hugs. Even Laura's husband, Jason, is getting used to it. "I'm just getting to like him more and more," I thought...and now I'm leaving. I detected a tear in my mother's eye. My sister was crying, but she cries more than anyone I know. My dad says it's her gift of mercy, which makes her an excellent special education teacher.

Ever been through the Amsterdam Airport? My route was Fort Wayne to Detroit, Detroit to Amsterdam, and Amsterdam to Manchester, England. I know how to negotiate airports. My parents had a goal years ago: Laura and I would each be able to get through any airport in the world – without help – by the time we graduated from high school. That doesn't mean we went to every airport in the world, it just meant that anytime we went anywhere by air, they would require us to find the next departure gate. It worked – as I found out. Traveling through Detroit was easy. It's a big airport, but nothing compared to my next transfer. I left Detroit in the early evening and flew across the Atlantic. The plane landed in Amsterdam the next day, mid-morning. The airport is huge. It's amazing to see the flight schedule board and all the destinations: New Delhi, Istanbul, Caracas, Sydney, Moscow, Stockholm, Nairobi, Dubai…Manchester, UK – that's me! I found my way – no problem.

The flight from Amsterdam to Manchester is short – under an hour. Instead of making me take the train from Manchester to Sheffield, some young adults met me at the airport and took me by car to my destination. I saw the church. It looked a little familiar. It had been four and a half years since the first time my dad took me. I saw Mick briefly. That brought back memories of how I got here. Wow – what a journey! Yeah, Mick sent an e-mail, asking me to apply. But long before that…I thought about that first trip. And, at the end, in Mick's living room, where he prayed. Where he put his hands on my shoulders. When he said, "I sense God has a word for you, Jon. I sense God is saying you'll be a mighty warrior for God." I thought to myself – I don't know if I want that guy to touch me again! I thought, "Let's see what I've gotten myself into first,"…or should I say, "what God's gotten me into?" Man, I am not sure I am ready to say that.

Then I think about how it all started – even before that. My dad hearing from God – in that same house, at Mick's breakfast table. Then how Dr. Bill made it possible for me to come. Then the dean in Florida encouraged me. Then Mr. Milton thought it was right. My parents were thrilled and encouraged me -- and my grandparents, my pastor, Laura and Jason. Man, I feel like they are all here as I step across this threshold into…I don't know what.

Chapter Twelve
Double Culture Shock

"Hi, my name is Tom," said the first FORM student I met at the house I would live in.

"Hi, I'm Jon," I said.

"Oh, you're the yank," Tom said, detecting my accent in a millisecond.

This began my cross-culture adventure. I lived in a house with four other guys. Some of the FORM girls had a house they share a few blocks away. This is the way they all live: in community. Just like a fraternity. I was already used to this. I loved my fraternity living. I thought, this ought to be easy. But, this was more than a fraternity where we were all studying for different careers; and, in my fraternity, many of us also played football. These guys were all Christians. More than that, they all wanted to learn more, go deeper, and experience authentic Christianity at a greater level – according to the website. I was not sure I was ready for that. I couldn't really explain how I got the courage to get there. I mean the spiritual part. A good part of it is that I had no idea where all this was going. I didn't want to become a fanatic – you know, like a monk or something. But the kids I met, when I was there before, weren't like monks. I counted on that. Also, Mick wasn't that strange. I still don't know about the "I have a word from God" thing – but he was a really cool guy. He'd become one of my dad's best friends. Dad wouldn't become best friends with a monk – I don't think.

The next day, we would start a retreat for orientation. I wasn't going to think about that. Some of the group in the house wanted to go out for a pub dinner and a "pint" of beer. (I was already learning a new language.) They ate, and they drank beer...in moderation, I'm sure – that's always a good sign. After the pub meal and some "English brew," I was sure I'd sleep well. I like sleeping. You don't have to think when you are sleeping.

We all pushed into two minivans and went out to a place in the countryside. It was beautiful. There were 14 of us in FORM: eight girls and six guys. Some of them grew up in that church, and others are from different places in England. One girl is from Denmark.

Our leaders were Dan and Jude, a young married couple. They were really cool -- not that old, but older than the students. Most of the students had just finished university. Some were taking a break in the middle of their university years. Some haven't been to university at all. They don't call it "college" in England. They called it university. So I had to learn to never tell people I just graduated from "college."

All these changes are called culture shock. My dad taught me about it when we traveled to other countries. Everyone experiences it. It can make you fearful, disrupt your sleep, and even affect your health. Your equilibrium gets thrown off, with so much that is different. You can have mood swings. I was glad I knew about this. Even though England and the United States have a lot in common, it's still a different culture. During the retreat, I already saw a different cultural thing going on, something that was affecting me more than the British culture. It's the Christian culture at a different level. Some of the other young adults were feeling it, too. I can tell. Our leaders are sensitive to it, and gentle about it. They were really great people – I could already tell. And the students were helping one another. That helps!

Part of it was language I had never heard before. They were talking about Christianity as a movement. I really like it, but I had always talked about church. They talked about phrases like the "person of peace," whatever that was. They said we were going to learn all about it. They talked about the language of Life Shapes®, as a way to think about discipleship. They promised that, little by little, we would become a part of this culture. They called it a biblical culture. I wondered why I never learned this before, it sounded cool.

FORM seemed to be a Christian type of boot camp. They were telling us that within 10 months, we would be equipped as high-end Christians. I liked that. I guess if you're going to be a Christian – why not be the best you can be? You know, like they say about the Marines. If you're going to live like a Christian at all, why go through the motions and play church? Why not do Christianity in a genuine way that really kicks butt for God? Actually, they did not say it that way, but that's the way I would say it. It's the way my football coach would say it. Maybe even a little more graphic!

"In the first part of the year, you are going to learn about how God uniquely made each of you," Dan explained.

I thought, "That sounds interesting. I wonder if I'll learn anything new?"

"Everyone has spiritual gifts," Dan continued. "These are supernatural attributes given by the Holy Spirit to every Christian."

"That's right," added Jude. "You will take a survey that will help you discover the gifts God has given to you."

I silently wondered, "Why didn't I hear this stuff before, like in Sunday school, youth group, or the pastor's preaching?"

"There will be other surveys you will take," Jude added. "You will learn your temperament, and you will find it exciting to use these discovery tools."

Dan jumped in with enthusiasm, "Most of all, you're going to spend the first half of the year doing all kinds of ministry. But don't worry, you won't be put in positions to fail or feel overwhelmed. You'll do it with people who already do these ministries. You'll have opportunities to find what passion God has placed in your hearts for serving Him and others."

Sally, a student from southern England asked, "What kind of ministries will we get to try?"

Jude was excited to list them: "You'll get a chance to work in a soup kitchen, work with those who are homeless on the street, minister to children and youth, work on university campuses...."

Dan jumped in, "You'll be working in cross-cultural situations with immigrants, visiting those in prison, have an opportunity to preach, share your faith...."

Jude came right back, saying, "We'll take weekend excursions to stay with Christians who are involved in special ministries, like service to the needy. We'll spend a weekend with Christians who used to be Muslims, and...."

Dan interrupted, "And we'll take a two-week mission trip to another country and serve the poorest of the poor."

"Then," Jude added, "as the year continues, you'll focus more on the ministry you feel God has called you to do. You'll find your niche! This will help you the rest of your life, whether you end up as a staff person at a church as a career, or become a missionary, or serve as a volunteer member of a church. You'll be ready and prepared, like most Christians have never dreamed."

I felt excited, and a little nervous. But, you know, even though I still don't know how it was going to feel – I already got the idea this is a special opportunity.

Chapter Thirteen
On the Streets

"FORM is focused on three objectives," said Jude, as we gathered for our first teaching day. "The first is to meet God. Second is to meet friends. Third is to live life better."

"That didn't sound so scary," I thought.

She went on to show a triangle. This was my introduction to a whole new and unique way of thinking about being a follower of Jesus. The three objectives make up a triangle, you know – with three sides. The points of the triangle are labeled UP, IN, and OUT. I had never heard this.

"Christianity is all about relationships," Jude continued.

"The UP is our relationship to God. It reflects our faith, worship, prayers, Bible reading…."

My mind wandered for a moment…back to the retreat. They handed out a Bible reading chart. During the 10 months of FORM, we read a part of the Bible – everyday! It was, like, several chapters. By the end of the 10 months, we'll have read through the Bible – the whole thing!

"That's a little spooky," I thought. In four years of high school and college, I never read that much. I always read the minimum. I don't like to read. But I thought I'd give it a try and see....

"The second part of the triangle is IN," Jude continued. "It's all about our relationships with other Christians. It focuses on how we treat one another. How we are willing to be open and vulnerable, and hold each other accountable. Not gossip – talk behind each other's backs – but speak to each other face to face, in love. It's about faithfulness to friends and our spouses, and...."

My mind wandered again. I have ADD, you know. The spouse thing got me off track. I had already met some new girls here. My new friend, Ben, was in FORM a couple of years ago and worked for this church now. Ben says FORM is a great place to meet girls. Ben likes girls. I made up my mind not to get into any relationships with girls during these 10 months. Heck, I'm only going to be here 10 months. Then I'd be back home. Having a girlfriend in England is way too complicated. Besides....

Jude caught my attention again: "The third part of the triangle is OUT. It reflects our relationship with those who are non-Christians. As Christians, we represent God to others. Our activities need to reflect our respect for God and our honor toward Him."

"I never thought about that before, ever," I thought. "Never in my life did that occur to me. I wonder why I…."

"We also are called to love our neighbor," Jude said. "We are going to learn a lot about serving others, especially the poor…."

"They have poor in England?" I wondered. "I haven't seen any poor people. How do you serve the poor? I have never done that. My church does a rummage sale each year and sells clothes and stuff cheap to people who, I guess, are poor. My mom cleans out my closet of stuff I can't fit into anymore. They make money to help run the church. I guess that helps the poor."

"The OUT also is about developing a relationship with those in need – being real people with them. We're always looking out for the person of peace, too…do you all know what we mean by that?" asked Jude.

Half our group shook their heads "no," including me. I figured it had to do with people in countries not at war, or people who didn't fight, or they lived peacefully, or something. I was wrong.

Jude explained, "The 'person of peace' comes from the directions Jesus gave to the disciples. Jesus was telling them to go into the towns, go door to door, and tell people about the Kingdom of God. If they found a 'person of peace' – you know, someone open to listening, ready to hear about God – then the disciples were to go in and spend some time with that person and share about Jesus...."

"Man, I hope we don't have to go door to door and talk to strangers," I thought.

"That's part of our OUT," Jude said. "If people show interest, we want to tell them about Jesus. If they don't, we figure it's not the right time in their lives." She continued, "Anyway, that's the triangle. It's the first basic LifeShape® we'll learn. There are others."

This was a side of Christianity that was new for me...and I liked it! I don't know why, but I had never thought of Christianity as relationships. All I knew is you went to church, did projects, raised money for youth trips, and went on these trips – like going to Cedar Point, an amusement park in Ohio. Our youth group did that every year.

Mostly, I thought of church as an organization. Churches are, like, institutions. You believe stuff and do stuff. It's like everything is about keeping the institution running. I guess I never thought about the Christian life being about relationships with God and other Christians. I especially never thought about the OUT thing – relationships with people who are not Christians. I mean, I have always had friends in school who didn't go to church. They showed no signs of believing in God. But I never.... I mean I didn't share my beliefs...and serving the poor, I don't really know what that's all about.... But I was soon to find out.

That afternoon we participated in an "OUT" activity – that's what they called it. We left the church at 3:30 p.m. We were hooking up with some church members who had a ministry to homeless people who hang out in the city center. (They spell it c-e-n-t-r-e. See what I mean about a different culture?)

"Are you kidding me? We are actually going to talk to bums on the street?" I thought. Later I found out that calling a person a "bum" in England is not a good idea. It's another name for "ass." Yeah, another part of my cross-cultural learning. But nothing compared to my spiritual experience with homeless people.

We went down to the city center with a group of church people who actually did this, regularly. At first, I didn't get it. Why would you go visit people, except to get them to come to church, become members, give money to the offering, to help pay the bills? These people have no money – and, by the way they lived, I didn't think they were going to come to church. So why bother?

We stopped at a grocery store and bought some food to give to them. "Don't they have, like government agencies where these people can get food?" I asked. I learned that there is never enough food, and some are not willing to go into the soup kitchens that operate here and there. I didn't know why.

As we walked up to the first homeless person, I was glad I was with someone who did this every week. I would have been petrified by myself. The homeless lady's name was Janice. What I discovered was amazing. She, like the others we would meet that day, was just like a normal person, just like anyone else. They were friendly. Most seemed pretty smart. They really appreciated the food. The only real difference with them is that they were homeless.

I was amazed at how these guys from the church knew these people and how the people enjoyed seeing them. They had regular conversations with them. Some were more open than others. The people from the church prayed with these people. Some...they even talked about Jesus. My eyes were really opened to a whole new world. It was just the beginning.

Chapter Fourteen
Life in the House

The guys I lived with were just regular guys. They weren't hyper-religious. They had some of the same questions as I did about God, faith, and the FORM thing. It was like we were on a journey together. I liked that.

I shared a room in our house with Andy. He went to secondary school (what we call high school) where he grew up – a place called Leeds. I wasn't exactly sure where that was – not too far by train, he said. People at FORM ride the trains a lot. It's a good way to get around from city to city. We didn't have that where I came from. Maybe in other parts of the U.S., but not in Indiana. We drove everywhere. In England, most young adults don't have cars. Many don't even have a driver's license.

Andy went to Sheffield Hallam University to study nursing. While he was in Sheffield, some young adults from the church met him in one of the clubs. The city has a lot of clubs. That's because there are many university students. The other big university is the University of Sheffield. The club scene is huge. On Friday and Saturday nights, the streets in the club district of the city are packed with young university students. Binge drinking is popular. There are a lot of drunk students on Saturday and Sunday mornings around 2 or 3 a.m. The church has a group that reaches out to students who are into the club scene. It's their mission, their OUT – like outreach. They go into the clubs around 1 a.m. and sit next to students at the bar. They try to start a conversation. If they find a person of peace, they'll talk with her for awhile. If the student is struggling with something – don't all students struggle with stuff? – they offer to pray for her. If the student says it's okay, they pray – right there on the spot! Then they offer to exchange contact information. That's the short story of how Andy ended up at the church.

You know, when I was in college – university – I spent a lot of time in bars. I did get drunk quite a bit. I never had anyone from a church come up and talk to me. I never saw anyone doing that in a bar. Never! I never heard of church people doing that, either. Have you?

The guys that do the club outreach are part of a "cluster." Andy was telling me about how they do it. It's a lot different than anything I've ever heard of. In fact, my dad says that very few churches he works with have ever thought of this idea. But, my dad says it is catching on in certain churches in the U.S.

I just thought that if a church is aggressive to get people, the first thing you would do is invite them to church, you know, a worship service. Andy said they don't invite people to church, unless they show they are really ready and eager to come. Most aren't. I'd say that's true of just about anyone I have ever met in bars in the U.S., too!

So, Andy said, they form what are called missional communities. They call them clusters. People in the church learn so much about God and the Bible, they get the mission thing. They understand outreach. Jesus gave His followers the "Great Commission" to go and make disciples. My dad is always talking about that. I figured that out when I was probably 8 years old.

Anyway, you belong to a cluster because you have a passion to reach a certain group of people and tell them about Jesus and disciple them. The group that met Andy is all excited about reaching students at clubs. There were dozens of these clusters at the church. They all had different target outreaches. Many people of the church were part of one of these clusters. One of the guys from a cluster reaching out to clubs – Joe – sat down, talked to Andy, and they exchanged contact info. Joe, then, connected with Andy a few days later and invited him to his cluster gathering. They met every couple of weeks at a pub and had a meal and fellowship. Andy went, met a lot of cool people, about 20, and had a good time.

The leader of the cluster asked about guests, and Joe, who invited Andy, introduced him to the group. Then the leader asked the Christians in the group if any had a story of how God did anything in their lives since they got together two weeks earlier. A few people shared, and Andy found out these people experience God in their lives.

This went on for several months. Andy liked hanging out with the group. He became interested in God. Joe, then, invited Andy to a Sunday evening service. It was a "cluster Sunday" and some of the clusters came and sat together. Andy said he would try it out. The rest is history. Andy became a follower of Jesus, and after university, he decided to stay in Sheffield – because of the church! Then he took FORM, and we shared a room.

"Hey," Dave stuck his head in the door of our room, "some of us are going to get together in the front room downstairs and hang out and talk about our trip down to the city centre to meet the homeless people. Do you guys want to join us?"

"Yeah, sure," Andy and I echoed each other.

You know, that was a great part of FORM. We lived together in community while we were on the journey. What a great idea. Jason brought his guitar – we sang some Christian songs. A year earlier, I could have never guessed I'd be doing that. It's too weird, but I actually enjoyed it. It's like life in Sig Ep, my fraternity. I loved fraternity life. FORM was similar. Much of this stuff I learned about Christianity was so new. And, I found it so interesting and challenging. But living in a house together – living in community – it was just so cool to be able to discuss stuff with each other. You found out the other guys were spooked out, too, about meeting the homeless people on the streets. You talked. You learned from each other.

When you think about it, that was the way Jesus equipped His disciples. Those guys – the disciples – had time with Jesus, did hands-on ministry, and lived in community, so they could get together and think about what they saw and learned. They could watch Jesus do ministry and later talk about it together and ask, "What was that all about?"

We all had duties around the house. "We learn to live in community," said Dan, one of our FORM leaders. "We learn to get along, solve problems, work out difficulties." It was a lot like my fraternity, except from a Christian perspective. It seemed to work.

Dan and Jude guided us to show respect to others in our house, to honor boundaries. We applied our faith to our living situation. It was good practice. It wasn't perfect. We had our challenges. I liked living with the guys – all except for laundry. British people are crazy! Most everyone has a washer to wash clothes. The washers are little things – the smallest I've ever seen. But hardly anyone has a drier, so you have to hang clothes outside to dry. You know how often it rains in England? All the time, practically! Well maybe not all the time, but it seemed like it! When it rained, you had to hang clothes all over the house.

We had a teacher who came to talk about prayer. I had never been involved much in prayer. My dad taught my sister, Laura, and me to pray spontaneously in front of the family. You never knew when he would call on you. He never warned you. I just always made it up as I went along. I really didn't know much about prayer when I showed up at FORM.

Chapter Fifteen
God Talk

I always thought prayer was kind of a private thing. You know, everyone kind of did it on their own. I never did much at all, mostly just when things were going really bad. My philosophy was sort of like this: If all else fails – if nothing else works, if you're desperate – pray. Otherwise, if you don't pray much, who is going to know?

At my church back home, the pastor asks for prayer requests. People who want prayer write a request on a piece of paper and hand it to an usher. Then the pastor gets these requests and talks about all the people who were sick or in the hospital, or whatever, and then he stands up there and prays – forever! I don't know how anyone can pray that long. I never know half the people he's praying for. Who can pay attention that long? I always thought the whole thing was boring.

At St. Thomas, they did something different. In church, Mick – the pastor (they call him a "vicar") – asked anyone who wanted prayer to raise his hand. The first time I saw that, I thought, "Yeah, right, who's going to do that in public?" To my surprise, a lot of people raised their hands.

Then he said, "The worship team is going to lead some songs – the words will be on the screen. Those who are Christians, gather around the people who ask for prayer, lay hands on them, and pray for them."

It was kind of an awkward moment – the first time I saw that. I was right next to someone who raised his hand. I didn't know what to do. Then, Mick said, "If you don't feel led to pray, you can just sing the worship songs, or just sit and listen – whatever." I wondered, for a split second, if the "whatever" part meant getting the heck out of there! But I stayed.

I was surprised. Several people got up and came over and laid hands on this guy. Someone asked if he wanted to share what he wanted prayer for. He didn't have to say, but he did. Then these people prayed for him...and prayed...and prayed. I bet it went on for five minutes. That's a long time to pray – don't you think? I mean, how much can you think up to say?

After church, they invited people who wanted prayer to come forward. They had a whole group of people up there to pray – not just pastors and staff. People knelt down and these guys laid hands on them and prayed. Sometimes they anointed them with oil. I've seen my dad do that. It's olive oil and they put a cross on a person's forehead. Sometimes people would shake. This went on for a long time. Some people collapsed – the first time I saw that, I thought they died on the spot. I was convinced – I'm not going up there!

Some people went up front after church and laid face down on the floor. It's okay – they let them do it. And whenever they got up, they got up. After my initial shock (which took several weeks), I just got used to it.

Every morning before FORM, we had morning prayers. Staff is there…and FORM students. Staff people prayed a lot. They must take a class in it at school or practice a lot. The students don't pray much. A couple do, but it's early in the year. Maybe that'll change.

At FORM, we had this teacher who talked about prayer. Her name was Anne. She was a "vicar," too. Anne spoke a little about prayer in the Bible.

"Prayer springs from a relationship with God. This has to do with our UP relationship – in the triangle. The stronger your relationship with God, the more you want to have conversations with Him," she said.

I never thought about prayer being a conversation. To me, it was more like a religious act or a church worship function. Then she started talking about prayer as a ministry.

"You see," Anne shared, "when you focus on prayer as a function of IN and OUT – for other Christians and for those who are not yet Christians – it becomes a ministry. When you pray for others, it is called intercession."

I'm beginning to see there is a lot more to Christianity than I've ever known. I've never learned. I grew up in a Christian home. I went to a church. But I was beginning to see that if you take a period of your life and just focus on living the faith....

"What's very exciting," Ann continued, "is healing prayer."

"Now this is spooky," I thought. I remembered seeing a pastor on television, back home, who was a faith healer. I thought that guy was a quack. And maybe he was. I figured it was trickery. But Anne was no quack. She wasn't doing this for money...or on TV. All the teachers who come to teach at FORM are volunteers – they even pay their own travel. There's nothing in it for them.

"Healing prayer is asking God to do a miracle," she said. "God intervenes. God wants people to be healed."

"Yeah, so why doesn't it always work?" whispered my skeptical brain.

"So why doesn't it always work?" she startled me.

"Does she read minds, too?" I wondered, half serious.

"You see," she explained, "we don't do the healing, God does. God knows what is best and when it is best to act. But to ask Him to heal is an act of faith on our part. It is believing God to do what the Bible says we are supposed to do. We can't just believe some parts of Scripture and ignore the parts that trouble our rational minds. God can't be comprehended, only believed."

That made sense, but I needed to think about that more. Why don't more Christians take it seriously?

After Anne left, we FORM students did our normal Team Time. Dan led the discussion: "What do you think?"

At first, everything was quiet. I wasn't the only one who had a challenge rearranging my worldview. I wasn't alone in all my questions about why every church doesn't take this seriously. Some of these other students come from churches where they only give lip service to this healing deal.

I thought about that the rest of the day. Something was going on inside of me. If I was going to be a Christian, I wanted to be a real Christian – not just go through the motions. I didn't want to play church. I wasn't saying my parents did, or my pastors, or my youth minister, Eric. But I did. I went through the motions: like practicing football. However, with the Christian faith, in some areas, I'd been sitting on the bench. I hadn't been in the game. If it's in the Bible, I want to do it. I want to be it.

That night, I looked in the mirror on the wall in our bedroom. Andy was downstairs with the guys. I looked at myself and did a reality gut check: "Who am I? Really?" I knew, then, I was changing. I was becoming…What? I don't know. But it felt good. It felt authentic. Real. It was as if I had God in my head all along, but then He was crawling down my chest and touching my heart. I think it was the relationship thing. It's kind of funny. I really liked it. I was in a different world. And it wasn't called England.

And my conversations with God? They were just beginning!

Chapter Sixteen
My Street Friend Sally

"There, I think I've got it," I said, mostly to myself.

"What's that?" asked Andy, who was looking over my shoulder at my laptop.

"I've been trying to install Skype, Andy." I'd been calling home on the phone, but I downloaded Skype so I could connect with my parents, and it would be cheaper. They bought a camera, so we could see each other.

Ever since I arrived at FORM, I had been catching up with my parents about every two or three weeks. I hadn't told them everything. I didn't know how. I didn't have the words. I'd never been on an adventure like this.

A few hours later, Andy was at the University of Sheffield campus, following up with a student he had led to Christ. The guy was a student from Egypt who was raised in a Muslim home. He was in England studying business and economics. Andy met him on a Love Sheffield Sunday.

Love Sheffield was when they locked the church on Sunday morning – about once every two months. No joke – they wouldn't let people in. There was no worship service. Instead, we put on these badges that say "Love Sheffield." They didn't say anything else, nothing about the church or the times of worship.

Everyone who came, met in the large downstairs room in the building next to the church. We all divided into groups – and you could have your choice: you could pick up litter, pass out water bottles, or give away chocolates. Sometimes we gave out flowers. It was hilarious! When you meet people on the street, sometimes they wanted to make a donation. We didn't take it.

Sometimes people ask, "Why do you do this?"

No, we didn't invite them to church or hand them a brochure about the congregation. We told them, "God loves us, so we share that love with others." Sometimes people wanted to talk more. That was maybe a sign that they were a person of peace. So we started a conversation.

Did we invite them to church, then? Heck no! We're taught that in a secular world, that's too big of a step. You can only get church people to do that – if they're unhappy with their own church.

Did we invite them to a cluster – a missional community? No, again. It was too early. Most people wouldn't be ready for that, either. So what did we do? We asked, "Is there anything in your life you would like me to pray for?" You know what surprised me? Many of those people who didn't even go to church, and know very little about God and the Bible, would tell you – a complete stranger – something you can pray for!

Then, you know what we did? Pray for them – right there on the spot. Right there on the street. If they showed signs of receptivity, we asked if they wanted to exchange contact information. That way, we could develop a relationship. If they were a person of peace, we might eventually be able to invite them to a missional cluster. That's how Andy eventually developed a relationship with this guy from Egypt – and introduced him to Jesus.

"Hellllllloooooooooooo," I greeted my parents on my first Skype call.

What a marvelous invention! I think about missionaries just 50 years ago – people so far away from their families, distanced by thousands of miles, waiting sometimes for months – just to get a letter.

"Hi, Jon," my smiling parents said in unison. "How's it going?" asked my dad.

"Yeah, it's good," I replied. "How's it with you guys?"

"We've got heavy snow right now. But we are doing okay," they replied.

"How's Mom-Mom and Pop-Pop?" I asked. Mom-Mom is what I've called my grandmother, on my dad's side, since I was first talking. My grandfather I call Pop-Pop. My grandparents live just down the driveway, on two acres of our family tree farm.

"Oh, they are doing fine," my mom shared. "Pop-Pop is holding his own." We had just put him into a nursing facility before I left for school. He had surgery for bladder cancer, and my grandmother couldn't take care of him. He was there, with the hope of regaining his strength, taking physical therapy.

"So what have you been doing?" asked my mom. Mom has always been so good to me. She not only handles the finances for the house and farm, but while I was gone, she also took care of my finances – on the U.S. side.

When I came to England, I was supposed to work three days a week. FORM was on Tuesdays and Thursdays, and we got Saturdays off. On Sundays, we had church in the morning and evening, and we often did some sort of ministry on Sunday afternoons. On Monday, Wednesday, and Friday, we all had part-time jobs. Why? It provided money for rent and incidentals. But the main reason was to be able to live and share your faith in a secular setting. You couldn't work at a church or some other Christian institution. You were supposed to be somewhere where you could practice your OUT.

My problem was, I couldn't earn money, because I was not a citizen. So I worked three days a week as a volunteer! I was there as a student. So, I had to raise money back home. I started this before I left. I spoke at church, sent out letters, and raised pledges for my support. The money went into my bank account back home. My mom took care of that. I used my credit card in England, and my mom paid off the credit card from my account. I sent thank-you letters to those who supported me. It was a faith adventure in itself. However, I think people got a lot back through my report letters. It's funny. I used to think it was weird that my dad raises his salary!

"So what have you been doing?" my mom asked again.

"Oh, yeah," I remembered. "I've just been writing a letter to report to my support partners. You won't believe what happened. It's the coolest thing. I have been hanging out with the homeless people in the city centre. They know me by name and greet me when I come to where they gather. They call me 'the Yank' because of my American accent. Anyway, around midnight one night last week, God spoke to me."

I couldn't believe I was telling a story about how God spoke to me. I remembered how weird it was when my dad first came back from England and God spoke to him about taking me to England.

"I heard God say to me to buy some bread and take it to Sally. God said, 'the lady will be sleeping on this certain bench by this fountain.' I knew the place. So I got Andy out of bed, and we went to the store, bought some bread, and walked down to the city centre at midnight. She was right there, lying on that bench! We gave her the bread. She was really hungry. We talked, and prayed for her."

"That's awesome, Jon!" my mother smiled.

"That's not all," I continued. "Last Sunday night, at the Sunday evening service, this homeless woman, Sally, showed up! I haven't got a clue how she got there. She uses a cane, and can hardly walk. She has no money for bus fare. She was all alone. Anyway, I spotted her at the beginning of the worship service. I went and sat down next to her. When it came time for prayer, she raised her hand, asking for someone to pray for her. I prayed for her leg to get completely healed. She said her leg got hot. Then she walked – without the cane! She was healed! It was awesome!"

I watched my parents as they looked at me. They were astonished. Not by the healing. They've seen that before in several places around the world. They were looking at me. To see their eyes was like looking into a mirror. I could see myself through their look. A teardrop trickled down my mom's face. Her son was spiritually ruined forever. And we all knew it.

Chapter Seventeen
Rainbow World

"Jon, take the ball, and play a game with the boys," directed Helen.

Helen worked with the children's ministry at the church. You could tell – she loved kids! I do, too. When I worked with the social agency while I was going to the university, I enjoyed the kids a lot more than I liked their parents. Of course, I was working for an agency that helped their parents see their kids under supervision, required by law. You know that can't be a good situation between the husband and wife. But the kids were always great.

My sister, Laura, is pregnant. I'm happy for her and Jason. They lost their first one – a miscarriage. That has to be hard – very hard. But Laura's doing fine this time. I am so glad. I pray for her, Jason, and the baby every day in my prayers. It's early in the pregnancy, but I am praying. In fact, I am praying more than I'd ever imagine. It's not a duty. It's just...

"Jon, are you and Franklin ready to teach the children the lesson about Abraham and Isaac?" asked Helen.

"Sure. Is it time?" I asked.

It was time. Franklin is another FORM student. We were helping out with the children's ministry for a few weeks. One of the great things about FORM is that we got to try different ministries. We were trying to discover our passion, our niche, the calling God has on our hearts. For two weeks, we visited those in prison. Having studied criminal justice, I found that to be especially interesting. At school, I had a very short section of teaching about interaction between social agencies and prisoners. That included chaplains. However, I never really gave much thought, at the time, to the role of ministry to prisoners.

By the middle of November, guess what I discovered? The whole world, including England, does not celebrate Thanksgiving when we do in the U.S.! Besides that, most of those who do have some sort of Thanksgiving celebration, do not eat turkey!

It's amazing how your worldview is shaped by your own experience in your own corner of the world. And, unless you learn otherwise, you think the rest of the world sees the world exactly the same way you do. And that just isn't so!

That's what FORM did for me, spiritually. It expanded my worldview. It stretched my worldview about Christianity, about church, about prayer, about ministry, about God, about me, about me and God, about people who don't know

God. About how to reach those who don't know God. About how to love those who don't know about God. About how to love those who are different from me.

Don't get me wrong, I wasn't turning into a religious fanatic or weird person. I still loved to joke, lift weights, listen to rock music, drink a beer...or two. I still loved American football. I tried to get used to English football (and not call it soccer). I still liked a pickup game of basketball – and I could really school those English guys! And I still love that! And I still don't like it when they school me at soccer...or...football. I still liked to hang out with friends and connect on Facebook, but I could feel myself becoming someone...not different...but...more. And I really kind of liked it. I really felt good about myself, and I really had no idea where this was going. And I was totally okay with that. I was...I don't know...content. Even though I was learning so much new...doing so much different. I had...I had peace. It sounds weird, but I had direction – even though I didn't know exactly where I was going.

Mick and his wife, Tricia, decided to have a Thanksgiving dinner for me – and invite the FORM kids – on the American day of Thanksgiving. And guess what? They had turkey, dressing, and pumpkin pie! Can you believe it? Some of the FORM kids had never had pumpkin pie. What incredibly awesome people are Mick and Tricia. And, Mick said we were going to call my parents, on Thanksgiving Day, and all sing..."God Save the Queen!"

You know what? FORM was fun. Christianity – real Christianity – is fun.

In my Bible reading one day, I was in Philippians 2. It said something like, "Your attitude should be like Christ's. Consider others more important than yourself." Mick and Tricia do that. The whole church does that. Christianity does that…if you learn it. If you live it. Do you think that would change our world?

"Jon, are you ready to go?" asked Dan.

"Yeah, let me grab my bag…give me a couple of seconds. I'll be right with you," I said.

We were off to experience hands-on ministry, cross-culturally. We had a teaching about missions to other cultures, and we were going to go do it.

"God made the rainbow. God made people of all colors, races, nations, tribes – ethnics," said our teachers, Bob and Mary. "The rainbow wouldn't be beautiful if it was all the same color. Neither would our world of people groups."

For some of our FORM students, that was the first time they would walk the streets with a variety of ethnic people. Oh, they all have been to Indian restaurants and know immigrant children who were in their schools – people from all over the world – but that's not the same as meeting them on their turf.

Fir Vale is an area of Sheffield that houses Middle Eastern and Eastern European people groups. The visit there was the beginning of our experience in cross-cultural ministries. The on-the-ground leaders were Joyce and Benson. He was a professor at the university. They were Nigerians who worshipped at our church. They were on fire for God. They moved into Fir Vale for one reason: to reach the people who live there and share Christ.

Joyce and Benson had an outreach to Eastern European gypsies, and Middle Eastern Muslims, from Saudi Arabia, Iran, Pakistan – places like that. It wasn't my first time for cross-cultural contact on a personal level. My parents have hauled Laura and me to churches in the U.S. that are Russian, African American, Latino, all kinds of churches. I've spent time playing with Thai, Cambodia, and Burmese kids in the Far East, and Zulu kids in South Africa.

I was a little more nervous about the Muslims we were going to meet in Fir Vale. Like just about any other fear, it dissipated quickly as you got to know the people. People are people. Some in every group are bad, but the majority love their children, want to earn a living, enjoy their kinds of music, are looking for answers in life, and need Jesus.

We learned about cross-cultural strategies. I was especially interested in the concept of planting churches: starting new communities of believers. I was inspired by Joyce and Benson. These people lived for mission to other cultures.

We learned this: Jesus was asked once about when would be the end of the world – when it'll come. He said there would be all sorts of things happen – like earthquakes and stuff. But that won't be the end. Then He said, "But when this good news is proclaimed to every tribe, language, nation, and race, then the end will come." It's like all history is connected with God's plan to save people. I never really knew that. Did you?

Chapter Eighteen
Home for Christmas

"Hey, Andy, when do you leave?" I asked.

"I've got a train leaving at half past seven," Andy replied as he pushed the last bit of stuff into his suitcase for Christmas break.

"What about you, mate?"

"I'm taking the train tomorrow at four for Manchester," I answered. "And then a 9 a.m. flight to Atlanta. I've got a three-hour layover there, where I'll clear customs. Then off to Fort Wayne. I'll be home tomorrow evening, Indiana time."

I was looking forward to seeing my family and friends. I was really glad my dad had lots of frequent flier miles so I could go home. I wasn't homesick. Life in FORM was busy – and exciting. I hardly had time to think about it. And, I'd talk to my parents on Skype every couple of weeks. My dad wasn't always home when I called. Sometimes he was on a trip, consulting a church. But my mom was always there. I think my dad was there maybe half of the times I Skyped them.

I looked forward to seeing Nick, Nate, Mackenzie, and Tommy. I also hoped to hook up with some of my college friends, like Dean and Black Jack. I kept up with a lot of these guys on Facebook.

I also wanted to see some people who supported me from my church. Dad asked me if I would have lunch with our pastors. They were curious to talk with me for some reason. Maybe they just wanted to know more about the church in England.

When I came out from security at the Fort Wayne Airport, there were my mom and dad, Laura and Jason, and my grandma. It was great to see them. Suddenly I felt something I wasn't expecting. I hadn't thought about it before. I felt a sense of accomplishment. I knew I wasn't anywhere near done. And I was glad for that. I was glad to be home, but couldn't wait to get back – even as I was arriving. Does that make sense?

But I sensed a victory. I had made it through two culture shocks: I got used to living in England and pretty much felt at home. And, I went through the most accelerated growth in my spiritual life I could ever imagine. What's more, I liked it. No, I loved it. I could have never predicted what it had been like. But – an even greater surprise – how much I enjoyed my place in life, with God, with myself. My dad said I glowed with confidence and contentment.

Our family is tight. FORM had been longer than any of us had been separated from the rest – ever. My dad's gone a lot, but he usually isn't gone long. Once he was gone for six weeks, teaching a big conference of pastors in South Africa, then flying to India to teach a big conference there. Another time, Dad and I were gone seven weeks. We were in South Africa for three weeks. That's when I shot the wildebeest, and then he taught the pastor's conference. And then we went to Europe, where our family toured all over for several weeks. I remember how much I missed my bed. But I was only 12 at the time.

After my taste of FORM, I had this strange feeling, like I had a foot in two countries – that I belonged to two worlds. How could three and a half months do that? Part of it was because I knew I was going back after Christmas. I felt like I was on a two-week vacation to my own home. Who goes home for vacation? It felt a bit weird.

Coming home reminded me of who I was when I left. As I settled into my old room, I sat on the bed and my eyes surveyed the shelves. A beer stein from Germany, a Michael Jordan poster, my football helmet from Tri-State, a few pictures, souvenirs from around the U.S. – all the stuff I left behind. It made me think of the me I left behind.

I was pretty unsettled when I left to go to FORM. I had no idea what I was getting into. It was a "leap of faith," but I didn't know if it was faith in God. It was more like a "leap-off-a-cliff-because-I-don't-know-what-else-to-do-with-my-life" faith. God works in strange ways to get your attention, doesn't He? I heard someone say, "Sometimes you have to go through the desert to get to the promised land." That's sure who I was – someone wandering around the desert.

Dad and I got a chance to talk during the third day I was home.

"What do you think about the state of the church?" he asked.

If he would have asked me that a year ago, I would have looked at him like he was joking. I would probably have said, "How should I know? You're the Church Doctor." But now, my head was spinning with thoughts. I didn't know where to begin.

"You know," I said, "I don't know a lot about many churches except St. John's. I mean, I have visited other churches with you and Mom, but St. John's is the only church I really know here. And, of course, St. Thomas' over in England." I thought about my answer carefully. "You know, I was pretty critical about our church before. I felt the worship was pretty boring. I think a big part of that was not the church, but me."

"What do you mean?" my dad asked.

"Well, I think my attitude was pretty immature. Kind of selfish. Yeah, they could use a worship leader – that would really help. But you know, I have always liked Pastor Bob and Pastor Paul. I have a lot more respect for them now. I have changed, not them. I don't think they have the training to know what to do in a world that's changed so much. It's not their fault."

"You know," Dad said, "they want to meet for lunch next week, after Christmas."

"Yeah, that's cool," I said. "I would love to spend some time with them."

"Jon, I have been looking forward to asking you a question," my dad looked real serious. "When I graduated from seminary, it was real clear to me what the number one priority is for a pastor. I think that all of us in my class felt the same way – all had the same idea about what was the priority."

"What was that?" I asked.

"Before I tell you," my dad said, "let me ask you. If you were a pastor of a church, what would be your number one priority – that you made sure you did every week, no matter what else was going on?"

"That's easy," I quickly reflected. "It's training up and equipping leaders."

My dad looked happily stunned and said, "We were taught that it was to prepare your sermon."

That seemed odd to me. In FORM, we learned that it was all about making disciples and equipping God's people for the work of ministry. My dad agreed.

We met the following week with Pastor Paul and Pastor Bob. My dad was unusually quiet. They asked dozens of questions, as if I was consulting their church. They were eager to hear my responses. Every time I said what seemed to be the obvious answer, they were more interested. It seemed strange. My dad said that what FORM was teaching me, and others, was a key to the future health and vitality of Christianity. He said young adults trained in the way I was being trained were the hope for the church. I told him that he was just biased because I was his son. He said, "No, this is a fact." Then he said that for the first time ever he felt like I was a son and more. He felt I was a colleague.

Chapter Nineteen
Authenticity

"Hey, Andy, how was Christmas?" I asked, as we hugged.

"It was great, Jon. My mom was sick part of the time, but she's okay now. We had a great time. How did it go for you? Was it hard to leave and come back?" asked Andy.

"Yes and no," I said, while I returned to unpacking my bags. "It was great to see my family. I hung out with my friends a little, too. And…."

"I bet that was fun," Andy interrupted with genuine interest.

"You know," I continued, "it was. But it was a little different."

"Like…how?" he asked.

"Well, my friends aren't practicing Christians. I still love them like always, and we had a great time. I was careful that I didn't come on too strong. And…well, I didn't want to give the impression that I thought I was better. You know?"

"Yeah."

"But it was just like old times, except...I don't know...different...a little. You know?" I paused.

"Yeah."

I didn't know if Andy really knew – from his experience – or if he was just sympathizing. Things were different – a little. I thought, "I am different. Not in a bad way, but a good way... different." I'm sure my friends could tell. But we still had a great time together.

Nate threw a New Year's Eve party. Most everyone stayed the night, as usual. I didn't drink much. I left at 3:00 a.m. I spoke in church the next morning at the 8:00 a.m. and 10:30 a.m. services. Yeah, I was tired.

"I'm just here for a couple of weeks," I told the congregation. "I just want to thank everyone who has supported me so far. I'm involved in a program for young adults called FORM. It's really cool. It's discipleship training. I'm learning so much about God, living as a Christian, doing ministry, and serving. I've really grown – just in a few months. I really appreciate your support. I hope you like my report letters. If anyone wants to support me...that would be great. I work over there part-time, but I can't get paid. So if you would like to help, that would be awesome. There's a sheet in your bulletin with more information. Most of all, I would really appreciate your prayers."

It was easy to speak. I didn't write anything out. I just spoke as God led me. I just prayed about it and spoke. I knew I was accountable to these guys who supported me. It's something we learned in FORM – the Christian life includes accountability.

"You want to join the guys downstairs?" asked Andy. My thoughts were suddenly back in England. "I think everybody's back from the Christmas holidays. Ben's here. They're talking about going down to the Old Grindstone and getting some fish and chips from the place next door. We can all catch up with each other about what everybody did during the break."

"Yeah, sure," I said. The Old Grindstone was a landmark. It was just down the hill from the church and one of the oldest pubs in the area. "Oh yeah, I'm back in England!" I thought.

I was glad to be back. I was looking forward to what was coming next in FORM. I was surprised how much fun learning about God and practicing Christianity could be, more like an adventure than a school. We were learning, but we were continually doing things to learn. And we were together – like a family, a fraternity, but with girls, too.

We were taught about an overview of the Bible. Our teacher was Rich. I'd met him before around church. He was a really cool guy. He was studying to be a minister. I'd been reading my Bible. I had kept up. Some days I got behind. I really got behind during Christmas break. On the plane back to England, I got caught up again. I used to just sleep or play games on planes. There I was – reading the Bible – for hours. I couldn't believe it! But I didn't want to be behind when we started up FORM again. Also, I knew we'd get asked about it in our weekly huddle.

Huddle is what they call our accountability group. I remember when I first started FORM and heard about huddles. It scared the crap out of me. I thought, "Man, if my mind wanders, and I see a girl, and have a passing thought, like 'She has nice boobs,' like, are they going to make me tell that and embarrass myself?" Yeah, I was scared about the huddle thing.

But it's not like that. First of all, they introduced us to the whole concept of accountability. They have a teaching that comes from the Bible. The key to a healthy Christian community and a healthy Christian life is to follow the New Testament guide to life: low control/high accountability. I'd never heard anything like that before.

What's funny, when I told my dad about this on Skype, I found out he figured this out years ago. In his work with churches, he helps them rearrange their church government.

He says the New Testament is clear about how churches should operate. But, he says, "Most don't. They operate just the opposite: high control/low accountability."

He says, "Churches have boards, committees, elections – all kinds of control mechanisms. Churches are worldly – run in worldly ways, not the biblical approach. And," he says, "They practice low accountability. Gossip is like a plague in most churches."

I asked him if they teach that to pastors at seminaries. He said he never heard about a seminary teaching low control/high accountability. What a mess for churches! I can see why accountability freaks out a lot of church people. I was freaked out at first, but as I learned, I found I love to practice accountability. It just makes sense.

On Tuesdays, in the afternoons, we had our huddle. The guys met separately from the girls. Good idea! We were led by Dan. Jude led the women. The leaders used the triangle there, too. They asked you how you were doing with your UP. That's when you were asked, "How's your Bible reading?" It's when you were asked about worship, prayer, your relationship with God. We went around and talked about it. For IN, we talked about our relationship to other Christians. We didn't gossip about them. We talked about how we were handling situations: solving problems, settling arguments, you know, things like that. I remember once I was having a problem with a guy in our house who always left his dirty dishes in the sink. "It's a boundary issue," Dan explained. Then he asked, "Did you go to him and follow Matthew 18? Did you speak the truth in a spirit of love? Did you avoid complaining to someone else – gossiping behind his back?"

"Yeah, we got it solved – the Bible's way," I was happy to report.

When we talked about OUT, we shared how our relationships were with non-Christians. One of our guys waited tables at a pub. His boss was a pain. Dan asked if he had prayed for him. That was a new idea!

In the church, anyone who was a leader – anyone who leads anything, was in a huddle. I know, the whole accountability thing sounds radical. But it's really not. The atmosphere was not judgmental, fearful, or dictatorial. It all focused on "speaking the truth in a spirit of love." It's in the Bible. I wondered, why don't more Christians practice that? Or even know about it?

Chapter Twenty
The Poorest of the Poor

"Who do you know that is poor? Really poor? Let's talk about it." Jude was introducing me to a world that would rock my world. She pushed deeper: "Anyone know someone who is really poor? Who do you really know, really well, who is really poor?"

When she put it that way, I had to admit – I really didn't know anybody. And never had. Have you?

You know, I've seen really poor people on T.V. Who hasn't? You know those commercials where they want money? "For $2 a day, you can feed this child." Then they show a starving kid, poorly dressed, no shoes, standing in the mud. For a split second, I would think about it. Then the commercial was over, and the next one was telling you to buy a luxury car. You quickly recover, get up, go to the kitchen to get a snack, so you can get back in time to watch the show you really want to see.

Isn't that kind of the way it works? It did for me.

I've driven through parts of Detroit and Chicago where there are really poor neighborhoods. You don't have to live in some strange place like Bangladesh to be hungry. They even have some here in England. Yeah, sure, there are the homeless. I had gotten to know them. But there are lots of people who have a home, of sorts, who are really poor.

"Jesus calls us to care for the poor," Jude says.

Sorry, but my first thought was, "Yeah, here comes the part where you want me to write a check."

"You know, many Christians care, intellectually, about the poor. They are compassionate, in theory, as long as they can keep the poor at arm's length." I could have sworn, she was looking at me. "Many Christians will write a check. That's good. It costs money to do any ministry. But a check is antiseptic. Sterile. It can be an intellectual commitment – and that's good. But it's rarely relational. It's not every Christian's calling to have a full-time ministry to the needy. Only some are called to that special ministry."

"Why do I get the idea 'but' is coming?" I thought.

"But," she said, "it's good for every Christian to rub shoulders with the poor. To touch, and feel their pain. To smell where they live. To hug their environment. To drink from their cup of suffering."

I was already feeling a little guilty at that point.

"This is not to make you feel guilty. That's not what Jesus does to motivate people. It is out of our love for God, when love spills over to our neighbors, all of our neighbors. Jesus – and New Testament Christians who live with Jesus in their hearts – have a special concern for those who are needy. The Bible talks about a special love for the poor, care for the widow, and concern for the orphan."

I had a feeling our adventure was about to go to a deeper level. To be honest, I wasn't entirely comfortable with this step on the FORM journey. But I was curious. Everything else had been awesome. I just needed to trust God. I was going to do that.

It's not a good idea to jump into a ministry you don't know anything about and have no experience or training. I'm glad Jude didn't just take us to a poor neighborhood and drop us off on a corner and say, "I'll be back in a few days to pick you up."

In every area of ministry experience, we came alongside people who were experts at doing it. Those people had experience – lots of it. They weren't just academics who taught in a classroom. They were on-the-ground people who get it, live it, know it, and do it. Dan says it's like an opportunity for God to stretch us. It's a time for us to find out if that's our calling, our passion, our interest. It's a taste of that ministry. But it's done with a safety net. We were surrounded by those who knew what they were doing. They watched out for us. You watch and learn. You help, and they guide.

I wonder why everyone doesn't learn ministry like this. Isn't it what Jesus did? What? We think we can improve on Jesus? Isn't that kind of arrogant?

Dan and Jude connected us with a mission well known for this work with the poor. They had been doing it for years. Our first experience was in Manchester. You know, you can fly into the airport there and take the train to Liverpool, Sheffield, or London…and many other places – and never see the poorer parts of the city. You can go to shopping centers and football matches and bypass these areas altogether. Maybe that's part of the problem: out of sight, out of mind!

England doesn't have the masses of poor like other developing nations. But there are many immigrants who have come to England. For those in the first generation, it's hard. Many have to learn the language. For them, the culture is extremely different. They don't always have the best education. Like back home in the U.S., England has employment challenges for those who have little education and few skills. There are some who come for asylum. That means they are fleeing persecution. In some cases, they are fleeing genocide – where a group in their homeland is trying to annihilate them. You don't hear a lot about that in the news. I don't think we like to think about that.

We stayed for the weekend at a shelter. We helped in the soup kitchen. We talked to the people. Some prayed for them. We delivered donated clothes and furniture.

At one place, we helped with repairs, fixing up these people's homes. I walked in the door with a couple of FORM guys and a couple of guys from the mission, and there was this woman who heard me speak.

"American?" she asked with a heavy accent. I think she was from eastern Europe.

It was cold and damp in the house. It was drafty in wintertime! Winter in England wasn't as cold as it gets in Indiana, but it was cold enough. It was too cold for the way that run-down house was built.

The people were so happy for help. Some of the guys from the mission started talking to them in another language. I couldn't tell what they were saying, or in what language.

When there was a break in the action, I asked one of the guys what he was speaking. He said, "Russian. These people are from an area of eastern Europe near the Russian border – a long way from here!" He knew these people. They helped them regularly.

They brought Bibles – in Russian. The people were so thankful. The lady had tears in her eyes.

Then the guy asked me if I wanted to pray for the family.

I said, "Hey, I don't know Russian."

He said, "Doesn't matter, God knows the American version of English, and Russian. I'll tell them the American wants to pray for them."

He rattled off some Russian. The people smiled and then they looked at me like they were ready to take it in like a sponge. Then they knelt down on the floor! I looked at the guy, and he nodded toward the floor and started to kneel. So I did, too.

"Oh Lord," I started without knowing where I was going with it. I just abandoned myself – not relying on my own understanding. I experienced something weird. I just prayed without thinking. I think I just got out of the way and it was like the Holy Spirit took over. I'm not even sure what I prayed – or what the Holy Spirit prayed…or….

Chapter Twenty-one
Working from Rest

Who gets the most out of it when you work with the poor?

This question continued to grow in my mind, as we had more experiences serving the poor in a variety of settings.

There were times when we helped out at a soup kitchen – just feeding the hungry. Or sorted clothes donated for children. We helped mothers and fathers pick clothes for their kids. We didn't always have the chance to pray, or give away Bibles. We just loved on people.

But the feeling was always there: a strange satisfaction or fulfillment. Like that was a healthy thing to do. It was kind of weird, but kind of the way I feel after working out. Yeah, I mean lifting weights. Except this feels better, stronger. It was almost like a vacation.

When you go on vacation, you get rest, and, if you get rest, you get energized. Working with the poor isn't taking a nap. It's hard work! But you feel energized. At least I do.

I'm not saying this is my calling or the passion God's given me for my Christian service. Working with the poor probably isn't my thing. I really don't know yet – I am still searching. It's not feeling like an instant, "Oh yeah, this is me." But I liked it.

Part of it is my love for people. Part of it is the need those people had. It was so obvious. I mean the people were hungry, cold, sick, suffering, needed clothes, wanted to work, needed education, training and skills, needed furniture and transportation, it just went on and on. And when you help, in any way, you know you've helped. God's used you to ease some suffering. It's a no-brainer.

I think there is a hole in everyone's soul. I don't know how to explain it. I think you try to fill this hole to get satisfied. I think you try to fill it with stuff. I think God put this hole there. It's to love your neighbor – serve people. It's the way we're wired. When you don't do it, the hole aches – like hunger pangs.

So you try to fill this hole with all kinds of soul junk food: sports, TV, electronic games, gadgets, beer, pizza, whatever. If you keep it fed, you can ignore it better – because it's preoccupied. But it is still there, and it's always asking for more. You're never quite satisfied.

I'm no Bible scholar, but I think God made us so we can't get this nagging hole satisfied until we give ourselves in service to someone who's in need. When we do, we feel satisfaction at a level you can't get in any other way. Doesn't the Bible say, "It's better to give than to receive?" I know that sounds like B.S. to most people. You don't hear many commercials like that. But Jesus says something about "when you do this for the least of these, you have done it for me," doesn't He? We had that teaching in FORM.

Think about it. Let's say Jesus is here right now, in the flesh. And you get who He is. Okay, let's say He asks you if you have something to eat. So you go to the refrigerator, and you get something. He eats it and says, "Thanks, that was really good. I feel much better." And you are there like, "I just fed the Son of God! I just satisfied the hunger of the King of Kings, the King of the Universe!" Holy shit…I mean, wow—can you imagine how that would feel?

Helping the poor just rings my bell. That's what my dad's friend, Wayne, would say. He probably would say, "Holy shit!" too. I don't mean to be disrespectful, but it's like a spiritual high. You know what I mean?

Life with God is so different than the world tells you about life. It's amazing. I'll tell you what…if I hadn't experienced this stuff, I would have never known this. I would have never believed it, either.

So you get energized working with the poor. Yeah. But it's no vacation. It's exhausting. Serving God is exhausting. If you are a living Christian, you need balance – and I'm learning that.

"Today we're going to learn about another LifeShape®," Dan said, as he drew a semicircle on the chalkboard. That was where we had our teaching. It was an upstairs room in a building next to the church, called the FORM Training Center. Trust me, it wasn't the high-tech, off-the-charts, impressive center of the educational universe. But you know what? It didn't matter. A lot of stuff I thought was important about churches – and life – don't really matter. I've changed my mind about this stuff.

What matters is people. People like Dan, Jude, and Mick, and all the teachers we've had. They "get it," and I get it from them. When you get it, who cares about all that stuff you used to care about? Christianity is all about people who get it and have a relationship with people who don't get it, but want to get it. Get it? It's all about relationships.

"So, what have you read in *Developing a Discipling Lifestyle* about the semicircle, Jon?"

"Huh? Uhhh…could you repeat the question?" I asked.

Dan repeated, "What have you read about the LifeShape® called the semicircle?"

I was back in focus. "It's about the rhythm of life," I said.

"That's right," Dan continued. "The semicircle reminds us of a grandfather clock with the pendulum going back and forth, back and forth. It's the rhythm of life, according to God's creation: rest/work, rest/work, rest/work."

This is the teaching my dad says convicted him so much. Any wonder. He works all the time. Well, not all the time, but he works way too much. He says he just loves his work. Mick does the same thing. He works so hard, too. Mick is the FDM guy: "Focus + Discipline = Momentum," he says. He says it all the time! I wouldn't be surprised if he has "FDM" tattooed on his butt, or some other place no one can see it.

"You know how Jesus always took time away to rest?" taught Dan. "There were always more people to heal, feed, teach. But He balanced His life. He got away from the crowds. This is called abiding time. Time to pray. Listen to the Father. Meditate. Time to retreat. Time to let the Father recharge Him."

Dan went on to talk about God's creation of the Sabbath – the day of rest. This balances life. Most people think of a weekend as the end of the week. What I am learning in FORM is different. The Sabbath is supposed to be the first day of the week. So, our world says, "Take time and rest from your work." God says, "Spend time with Me first, put Me first. Don't rest from work, but work from rest."

I know, you're saying, "What difference does it make? It is still a day you take off, whether you call it the first day of the week or the last." Right? Wrong! Let's say you are going on a business trip overseas. You work like crazy to "get everything done." The last night you stay up late packing. You leave the next day exhausted and start out all tired out. But, if you practice the rhythm of life, you'll get everything done two days before you leave. Then, you'll spend the day before you go resting, abiding with God. You'll leave refreshed. And you'll probably live longer. You work from rest. That's what we learned about the semicircle.

Yeah, this FORM stuff is changing the way I live.

Chapter Twenty-two
MentorTom

"Hey, J-Dog, are you ready to go? We're going to be late for breakfast," shouted Andy.

"Yeah, give me a minute to brush my teeth. We'll make it," I said.

We had breakfast together – all the FORM students – every Tuesday morning. We also had lunch together on Thursdays. It wasn't just a way of expressing our community – although that was part of it. It was also part of our learning in the area of service and hospitality.

This was how it worked. FORM provided a certain amount of money – a budget – for each breakfast and each lunch. Each of us were assigned to a group to provide breakfast or lunch. There were three of us in the group. We had to work as a team, make a shopping list, go to the store, stay within budget, get to FORM before everyone else, make breakfast, serve breakfast, and make sure everyone had enough to eat.

I discovered I like to cook! I must have gotten that from my mother's genes, certainly not from my dad's. Anyway, that was part of the FORM experience. We served each other, whenever it was our turn. We learned to get the most out of the money budgeted. There was also a little competition to see who could improve from what the other teams had provided.

You probably know most church people like to eat. Churches are always having dinners. People gather in small groups in homes to study the Bible – and eat. Youth groups have dinners and bake sales. When you think of it, a lot of Christian fellowship happens around food!

Tricia, Mick's wife, is a gourmet cook. Anytime you're invited to their home for dinner – go! She is an awesome hostess, and the food is fantastic. I don't see how Mick can be so skinny.

Tricia taught the FORM class on service and hospitality. When you think about it, with all the cooking and eating that goes on in churches, you'd think that this would be a required course for church membership!

Tricia taught us about the art and ministry of service and hospitality. Did you know there's a passage in the Bible that says you should "open your house to strangers and treat them well because they may be angels in disguise"? I never thought about having guests over as a ministry. But it is. Back in Indiana, our house is pretty big. That's good because, in my dad's work, he knows lots of people – from all over the world. These people come and stay all the time. Sometimes I had to sleep on the floor – and I wasn't very happy.

It's not that I can't sleep anywhere – I can. But I thought it was rude to push me out of my bed for some lady from Taiwan. I had no clue this was a part of Christian ministry.

Of course, I had plenty of parties at my house during high school and even college. We had guys sleeping everywhere. Our house was like a hotel some weekends. Laura had girls over sometimes, too. Once, during one of the summers I was home from college, I had a party – and was that a party! My parents were in China and Tibet for five weeks. About 300 people showed up at our house. People invited other people who I didn't even know. We got a couple of holes in the wall by the kitchen. I'm not sure how. Also, someone broke the toilet in the basement – cracked the bowl. It must have been one of those linemen from the football team. Those guys were really big!

Yeah, I have practiced a little hospitality in my day, but not always for Christian reasons. The FORM teaching put a whole new slant on the idea of entertaining others. And it's in the Bible!

Some people think Christians don't have fun. That's just wrong! Jesus made wine out of water at the wedding at Cana – and that was after the first batch ran out. It was His first public miracle. How cool is that!

The whole church at St. Thomas seemed to know about the Christian concept of service and hospitality. FORM students were regularly invited to a meal at someone's home. Can you imagine what a fun place that church is?

We made it to breakfast just in time. One of the boundaries they talked about at the beginning of FORM was to always be on time. It's the way we show respect for each other – something I learned. Now, I hate to be late.

But if you have a problem, are late, and apologize, people forgive you. That's respect back. If the whole world operated like this, what kind of better place would it be?

"Hey, Andy, how are you?" asked Sally. "Hey, J-Dog, how are you doing today?"

"I'm doing great, how are you, Sally?" I asked.

"I'm well, thanks," she replied.

I got the name J-Dog from Tom. Somehow it stuck and spread. The "J" stands for "Jon," of course. I'm not sure about the "Dog" part. In informal settings, my friends called me "J-Dog." Not long ago, I changed my e-mail account. Ben suggested I add FDM to it. Guess I got my dad's genes there – or it rubbed off from Mick – who knows? Anyway, that's me, J-Dog FDM!

Tom was my mentor. He was, like, the assistant pastor to Mick. They called him a "curate" – whatever that means. He was one of the funniest guys I had ever met. He and his wife had a house full of cats. I'm glad he didn't call me "J-

Cat." I grew up with a dog on our farm. Her name was Jenny. I picked her out as a pup and named her. We grew up together. I buried her when she died. We had a lot of good times. I would like a dog again someday. I don't mind being called J-Dog.

Every FORM student had a mentor. They were the same gender as you – an older, more mature Christian, who has had more time with God on the journey. Tom and I met about every two weeks.

When we met, our discussions were confidential – just between us. We could talk about anything. Mainly he wanted to know how it's going. Tom wasn't part of the FORM leadership.

Sometimes Tom and I went out to get something to eat. Occasionally, they had me over to their house. Sometimes we met at his office. Sometimes we sat outside, when it was nice.

As a mentor, Tom was a safe person – a safe place for me to talk about anything. He was a good listener. Most of all, he was an awesome encourager. He always cheered me up, even if I didn't need it.

I got a lot of wisdom from Tom. I guess that's what mentors are supposed to do. He always gave me good advice. At the beginning of FORM, it was a challenge for me. You know, living in another country. And, FORM stretches you a lot – at least at first. It isn't radical or extreme, but you learn so much about the Christian faith that you never knew before. And you are experiencing so much that you've never experienced before. The mentor concept is a great idea.

Tom also reviewed the triangle with me, almost every time we got together. He asked about my UP – my relationship with God. He asked about the aspects of UP – my worship life, prayer discipline, Bible reading. He asked about my IN – my relationship to other Christians. How I'm getting along with other FORM students, whether I'm in good communication with my parents, staying connected with my support partners, praying for my pastors, in England and at home. He asked about my OUT – how I was doing with those who are not Christians. Was I developing relationships with people of peace, serving those who are not believers? My OUT, to be honest, was my weakest part. But that was about to change!

Chapter Twenty-three
My Campus Call

Tom and I met at the coffee shop, just down the hill from the church. It was one of our mentoring sessions. It was a Wednesday morning, and I was due at work in about an hour and half.

I work like all the FORM students, at a part-time job on Mondays, Wednesdays, and Fridays. That's part of the FORM life, to work in the world. That is where you had an environment to practice your OUT. The money you earned helped pay rent, buy clothes, food, and other incidentals.

Of course, I couldn't make money in the U.K. Since I grew up on a tree farm, and since I still lift weights and am strong in my arms and shoulders – I work for people who need trimming and yard work. Some of them donate to the church and that helped pay my tuition cost for FORM because it added financial revenue to the church. The donations were completely voluntary.

"Hi, Tom," I greeted, as I walked up to his table. "What are you drinking?"

"Hey, J-Dog, how are you?" he said. "I'm having a latte."

"Mind if I get one?" I asked.

"No problem, man. Can you bring me a spoon?" he replied.

"Sure will," I said as I walked toward the counter.

We had our usual mentor talk. It was great, as usual. Tom was a wonderful man. I could tell, though, he had something else on his mind.

"Jon," he said.

I knew something strange or unusual was coming. How? He called me "Jon" for a change. It's like when my mom called me "Jonathan" instead of "Jon." It meant I was in trouble for something. Tom caught me by surprise.

"Mick and I have been talking," he said. I thought, for a moment, I did something wrong, but couldn't think of anything.

He continued, "We think you have some special gifts. We especially think you have an affinity for people and the gift of leadership. We think God has a call on you to be a leader. Have you ever thought about it?"

"Not really," I said. I can plan a great party for 300, but I don't think that's what he had in mind – or at least it's only slightly related.

I did remember my dad saying, on several occasions, that he thought I had the gift of leadership. I figured he was just biased because he was my dad. I blew him off, because I thought he was projecting his own dream on me. I didn't take it seriously.

My dad is a great fan of John Maxwell, a Christian guy in the States who writes and teaches on leadership. In fact, they are friends. Every time Laura and I got in the car with my dad and we were on a trip of more than, like, an hour, he would play a John Maxwell CD on leadership. Even when we went on vacation. That's my FDM dad! It used to drive us nuts!

"Yeah, we think you are a leader for God," said Tom again. "You have a lot of influence on others. We think God may use that. We want you to just think and pray about it."

"Yeah, okay," I said, "I'll pray about it. I guess I can do that." I didn't think much about it after that.

After our meeting, I went to work at this guy's house. He had a hedge to be trimmed. It was huge. It rained a fine mist most of the day. Welcome to England! No big deal. I've been wet before. It rains on the tree farm in Indiana, too.

On Thursday, we had a great teaching in FORM about growing the Kingdom. We talked about witnessing our faith, reaching out to others, planting churches, and developing Great Commission strategies. It reminded me of the frequent talks our family had at the dinner table when I was growing up.

That afternoon, Jude briefed us on our next ministry experience. "Today, we are starting another OUT experience for your group. We are now finished with the ministry to secondary school students. Everyone have a great time with that?"

Yeah, I enjoyed that. In fact, I thought the outreach to what we in the States call high school students might be my niche.

"But now," Jude explained, "we are going to focus on outreach to university students. At 3:00 p.m. today we are going to have a commissioning for you guys to go out."

We always had a commissioning for our outreach ministry. It included a great time for worship and praise. Then we had time for prayer where we just gave ourselves over to God. It occurred to me how natural that had become in our lives. When we started FORM, seven and a half months earlier, none of us had a clue. The first time we were commissioned – to go out to the homeless people – it was silent. Nobody prayed. Now everyone was really into it. Wow – we had come a long way!

Then Dan and Jude laid hands on us as we knelt down. They prayed God would lead us to find students who are people of peace – ready to hear our personal faith story or let us pray for them or exchange contact information and start a relationship. Then they prayed God would anoint us with His Holy Spirit to be ambassadors for Christ on the campus of the University of Sheffield. That afternoon, we invaded the campus for God! We went with those from the church who had formed a cluster – a missional community – to reach university freshmen. They knew the campus. They knew how to talk to students. They were good leaders and guides for us in that area of mission.

About 94 percent of the university students in the UK register for school and choose not to check the box that asks if they are Christians. Of the other 6 percent, 90 percent of them are nominal Christians – in name only. They check the box, but have no relationship with Jesus. They were probably baptized as a family ritual, but most of them have never been to a church since, except for a wedding. We had a great experience. Almost immediately, I felt this was it for me. My calling could well be, at least at that point in my life, to reach out to university students. I thought, maybe, when I went back home, I could help part-time at Trine University, my alma mater in Indiana. Maybe I could volunteer for a church that wanted to reach those university students. Little did I know!

Chapter Twenty-four
Worship White Hot

"Elle, that was a good breakfast. Thanks! Your group did a great job. Those bagels were amazing," I said. I just wanted to compliment them on the good job.

"Yeah, thanks, Jon. You get enough to eat?" she asked.

"Oh, yeah, it was great. Thanks!" I returned.

"J-Dog, did you get your Bible reading done last night?" asked Andy.

"Yeah, why do you ask?" I wondered.

"Because when I saw you last, you were asleep in the chair," Andy laughed.

I laughed, too. "Yeah, I fell asleep somewhere in Ezekiel," I said. "I finished it this morning."

"Hey, guys, before Team Time is over, and Becca starts the teaching, let's talk a little about Zurich, okay?" asked Jude.

Team Time happened after breakfast and after every teaching. It was a great time to catch up with each other. We were like a family. We will be a family no matter what, no matter where we are, for the rest of our lives. Some of those young adults are going to marry each other, I predict. Right now, everybody was focused on FORM, pretty much. And that's the way it should be. But I saw some electricity going on between some of those young adults. Oh yeah, give it a year or so and I can think of some of those students hooking up.

There was a girl in the church being extra nice to me. She was not in FORM. She was a student at the University of Sheffield. But she was a friend of some of the FORM girls. She was from Liverpool. Ben, who seemed to know everything about who knows who at the church, said she had her eye on me and wanted to get to know me. I said Ben was full of beans.

Her name was Esther. I had talked to her a couple of times. She was beautiful. But I had no plans to get connected in a relationship with any British girl. It would be too complicated.

"About Zurich," started Jude. "Dan and I have completed our arrangements with Networks. This is the ministry in Zurich where we are doing our two-week, out-of-country mission trip next month. Make sure your passports are up to date and your work arrangements are covered for being gone for that time. In a couple of weeks, we'll have a briefing. You're going to be working the streets with Networks ministry people, reaching out and sharing your faith in the red light district of the city."

"Does this mean what it means back in the U.S.?" I wondered. Where I came from, that's where prostitutes hung out.

Jude continued, "Zurich is an international city. People from a great number of nations come there on business. Many visit the red light district. As you might imagine, most of them are not Christians...."

Some of us softly laughed, probably to relieve a little tension.

"So you can imagine what great opportunities we will have to share Jesus Christ," Jude continued.

Dan added, "Begin praying for God's anointing on our work there. We will be bringing you more updates."

I had to admit, when I thought about Switzerland, I just thought about skiing. I love to ski. I couldn't imagine what it would be like in Switzerland, on those mountains. Most of the skiing I'd done was in northern Michigan. It's great to ski there, but they don't have mountains like Switzerland. But the mission challenge did sound exciting.

Becca took over the front of the FORM Training Center room and began teaching us about worship. Becca is the worship leader at St. Thomas, Crookes. She is an awesome, gifted worship leader.

Worship in the U.S. is the main attraction – why many people end up at the church they attend. People shop around until they find a worship service that dazzles them. The interesting thing about the way this church operates is that it doesn't grow through dazzling worship. It grows because people are constantly going out and reaching out to unchurched people. This is what they taught us.

The Great Commission says to "go," but for most churches the strategy is to invite people to worship. In Sheffield, people do things like Love Sheffield. Everyone is a missionary, developing the relationships in their networks. And most are involved in a missional community – a cluster. They are out there, looking for the person of peace, focusing on the club scene, university students, young families, and certain neighborhoods – estates, as they call them here. They invite the person of peace to their cluster gatherings, which are held away from the church, and share their stories of faith. Eventually, many will come to church. And they do, in great numbers. And when they do – guess what? There is dazzling worship! Mick calls it "white hot worship."

Becca taught us that they work hard to make worship here engaging. Mick has a way of making everyone feel at home and welcome. I liked when it was "cell phone time." He did this often, in worship. He'd say, "Take out your cell phones." The first time I heard that, I thought he was scolding us and going to tell us to turn them off. No way! He said, "Take out your cell phone. Text someone you know, who may not be a Christian. Tell them you are in church and having a great time. Tell them to have a great day. It doesn't matter if they're sleeping. They'll get the message when they wake up." After he said that? That's what everybody did!

Also, there rarely was an offering. Most everyone gave to the offering by direct deposit. If you wanted to bring an offering to the front, there was a time for that.

Worship at St. Thomas' was engaging in other ways. Everyone who led worship, not just Becca, but the whole band – anyone who was up front –led engaging worship by the words they said and more. They showed they were engaged by their body language. They modeled the way the rest of us should be worshipping. That's real leadership for worship.

Worship was interactive. It wasn't just the cell phone thing. Becca led, and other leaders did it, in ways that drew in your participation. That's why they did the prayer, involving the people through laying on of hands, praying for others. It was all interactive.

Even the preaching was interactive. Mick had a wonderful way of sharing the message. He was spontaneous and funny. All of that engaged people through their participation in the message. He'd ask questions and ask you to raise your hand. He'd occasionally refer to someone in the congregation. He told stories. All of that made it easier, even for me, to follow along.

The preaching and teaching was not Christianity-light. It was solid, deep, and direct. They didn't have to water it down for newcomers. The church was not a church of attraction. The missional communities attracted and matured new believers.

"Worship is all about God," said Becca. "But it's also about you, the worshipper. Much of what you get out of worship has to do with your relationship with God."

I thought a lot about that. I thought about the problems I had with worship back home at my church. A good part of that was me. When you have a church that disciples people – where people grow in their personal relationship with God – you are going to have white hot worship.

I had grown so much. I had become such a different person. I now came to worship with great anticipation. Heck, before, I just showed up. And I had an attitude, like, "What are you going to do for me?"

FORM has even changed the way my home church does worship – for me. Because I am a different person. When you get a whole congregation of people in worship who are on fire for God – yeah, it dazzles. When the Holy Spirit shows up, He is not just in the band, or worship leader, or preacher, He is in the people. He is in me. No wonder I now think worship is so much fun!

Chapter Twenty-five
Zurich: Red Lights and God's Light

"You know, I think she likes you," said Ben.

"Oh, come on, Ben, you're crazy," I answered.

"No, J-Dog, I'm sure she does. You need to ask her out," he continued.

I finally went out for coffee with Esther. We had a nice talk. Yeah, she was beautiful. She was nice. She was smart. She was a sold-out Christian. She was British! Why hadn't I been able to find a girl like this in the U.S.? Maybe it was because I wasn't attending church much the last couple of years. I thought, "When I get home, I might look for a church with a lot of girls my age." How's that for a reason to pick a church? Heck, I couldn't think about that right now because I was focused on FORM.

Actually, I was focused on God – probably for the first time in my life. I wasn't worried about girls all that much, or my future, or what I'd do after FORM. They taught us: the Bible says, "All things work together for good, for those who love God." Sometimes, when you quit trying to do everything yourself and just rely on God, things work out better anyway. Yeah, I was focused on God. A byproduct is peace. I liked that. Know what I mean?

I had also found my niche, at least for now. I loved working with university students. I'd been working on the campus at the University of Sheffield with some of the guys from the cluster that reached students there. They also had me working a little bit with students in other areas of the church. That seemed to be where God wanted me at that moment. I think that's my passion. At least at that point, that's what I really liked.

I felt more sure about life. I don't know how to explain it. Directed. Even though I didn't know what I'd do when I got home, I just sensed God had a plan. Is that crazy?

I was becoming more disciplined. What's up with that? I seemed to be more organized. I was more intentional about my life. Did I just finally grow up? Nah, it's not an age thing. I think I just grew…. What? Matured? Not really. I don't know. I think…I think it has to do with growing in faith. Who would have ever guessed? Okay, I had grown spiritually. Is that what people mean when they say that? Who knows?

I felt like my faith was on a roll. I had no clue where, or what. But you know what – it didn't matter. I had this sense that whatever God had in store for me, whatever that was – it would be okay. It was kind of liberating.

Back when I was in school, I felt...I don't know...trapped. I signed up for criminal justice, took all the courses. But...it didn't feel right. I partied. I slept a lot. I didn't want to think about it. You know, the future.

After FORM, I didn't have that issue anymore. I jumped out of bed in the morning – eager to tear into life. Experience it. See what God has in mind. Knowing God is like a wake-up call that jumpstarts life. It, like, gives you momentum.

Wait a minute. Momentum? FDM? Focus + Discipline = Momentum? I didn't see that coming! No wonder my friends said that about me. Oh crap – I just became my dad!

No I didn't. I'm not him. I'm me. But I have the enthusiasm like Mick, and my dad – for life. For God. For God's work. For those who don't know Jesus. Is that what it's all about?

You know, like my youth pastor, Eric. He's that way. So is my dad's friend, Roger. Actually, so is my mom. For that matter, so is my sister, Laura, and my brother-in-law, Jason. I mean – everyone is different. They all have different personalities, but they are all sold out for God......have momentum. So does Tom. I've seen it in Andy, and the other FORM kids, and Becca, and Jude, and Dan. How come I didn't see that before?

"Jon, here's a note from Tom," said Dan. "He dropped it off this morning." I read the note: "J-Dog, God's power be with you in Zurich. Let's hook up when you get back. Mick and I would like to meet with you sometime. We'll make an appointment through Dan and Jude, after you return. Keep your eyes off the red lights in the red light district. Love you man, Tom."

"Smartass!" I smiled. "That's Tom – always a sense of humor. I wonder, why do they want to meet with me?"

Jude and Dan were at the front of the Training Center room. "Hey guys," said Jude. We have some last-minute details to go over before we leave for Zurich tomorrow."

I couldn't believe it was time for our mission trip. Where did this year go? We landed in Zurich on a bright, sunny day. What a big city! From the air, it looked large and a little intimidating. I didn't understand how God could use a few FORM students to do anything there.

We met the guys from Networks. They've had a ministry to this city for years. They were from several different countries. As Christians, they're brothers and sisters of a family that has no boundaries.

"Everything we do is by building relationships," said Bob, one of the leaders. "We are glad you're here. We appreciate the help. We see Zurich as a great big platform – a stage – to reach people for Jesus. There are those who call this city their home. There are others who are short-term visitors. They come here for business from all around the world. Zurich is like a crossroads of commerce on a global scale. We reach people for Christ who leave with changed lives and go back home to dozens of other countries taking this new faith with them."

Another Networks leader spoke up. "My name's Anthony. I'll be your guide on the ground and your coordinator for the time you're here. We'll get you settled in and, today, we'll hit the streets for Jesus. Let me pray for you...."

By the time he finished, I was about ready to wet my pants with excitement. I was ready to take this city for God. His prayer was like a religious version of my football coach, just before a game – except with much better language. I learned you can have a good pep talk by praying. Imagine that!

Each day we learned more about the ministry Networks was doing in the city. They helped the poor, assisted travelers, and did hard-core witnessing on the streets. I was amazed at how confident these guys were – and they could begin a conversation with just about anyone – in a city where you can find 100 different languages. But, many people spoke English as a second language. Those of us who speak some brand of English have quite an advantage for God's work around the world. Ever think about that?

As the days went by, the Networks group involved us more in witnessing and service. It is amazing what God will do using willing servants – even newcomers who don't know much about what they're doing.

One day, Paul, one of the Networks guys, and Andy and I were walking the streets in the red light district. We started up a conversation with a guy who knew almost no English. He was an Italian, here on business. We didn't ask why he was in the red light district, for obvious reasons. I couldn't say for sure, one way or the other. But, surprise! He was really receptive. He was, at that moment, definitely a person of peace. His business was doing poorly, and it was like he wanted to talk. I didn't know Italian, but I had some Spanish way back in high school. That was close enough, so we could talk. The Holy Spirit showed up! I led this guy to receive Christ into his life using my half-forgotten Spanish! Talk about miracles!

Chapter Twenty-six
The Journey to Ecclesall Road

Zurich was an incredible two weeks. People were healed, several came to faith, we helped the poor. We got a glimpse of what God could do in tough places – anywhere in the world. God is just looking for people crazy enough to go and trust Him to use them. People crazy in love with God.

Networks is not the only ministry in Zurich. Only God knows how many there are. It makes you wonder how many thousands of ministries exist around the world, each one with a special niche – born out of the vision of some leader, and focused on some target of people Jesus died for.

All these ministries need help – for weeks, two years, or a lifetime. It's like this underground movement with all this ministry. You fly into a place, like Zurich, look down at this sprawling city from the air, and who knows how many ministries are working there. God knows!

I was pretty sure I wanted to serve God. Out of the ministries I had tried so far, I wanted to continue to hook up with some ministry that works with university students. I had been working, as I said, with the students at the

University of Sheffield. I wondered how many thousands of ministries all over the world do that work. It's like a gigantic job market just under the radar. It must be huge. How would I tap into that? I decided to think about that when I got home – there was only one more month of FORM.

When we arrived back in Sheffield, we were exhausted and exhilarated. What a trip! It had been an experience I'll never forget. I wondered if I'd ever see that Italian businessman again. I wondered if I'd see him in heaven.

One thing surprised me a little. I was looking forward to seeing Esther again. When I called her, she was eager to catch up with me, too. She wanted to learn all about the trip to Zurich. We decided to have dinner Wednesday night.

Esther's family was very involved in a contemporary-styled church in Liverpool. Even though England is a secularized country, there are pockets of on-fire Christians. Esther's family had always been mission-minded. Before university, Esther took a year off and went through discipleship training at a base operated by Youth With a Mission in southern France. For her outreach, her group went to Mongolia.

She had always been interested in France. At the University of Sheffield, she majored in the French language and French history. She had her final exams coming up in a few weeks.

"Everyone recovered from that great mission trip?" Dan asked our FORM team. "Did you have a great time?"

To a person, the entire team erupted with clapping, whistling, and yelling – no lack of enthusiasm in this group!

"Today our guest teacher is Helen. She is here to teach on family," said Alan. "Anyone here not from a family?" It was a joke.

Helen was awesome. She led us through a questionnaire about family. It asked all kinds of questions about the way we grew up. It was a reflective exercise: Who cooked? What did you wish your mom did more? Less? Was the toilet seat usually up? Down? All kinds of questions. She predicted that many of us would be married someday. And have kids. It was almost too much to think about.

"What should a Christian home look like?" She asked. "How is it the same as other homes? Different?"

We had a lively discussion. It was very good. It made me think a lot. She made us think of all the different ways people do family and the different roles mothers and fathers take. The shared duties. The unique tasks based on gifts and interests. It seems like everyone should spend a couple of days talking through this stuff before you get married.

Esther and I had a great meal. We went to the Thyme Café in Broomhill, not far from the church. It's a typical English pub atmosphere, with awesome food. We had a glass of wine. Then another. I could really come to like her. I don't know, she seemed…special. But we were worlds apart with a big Atlantic Ocean between us. I just kept saying to myself: "It's too complicated. Keep it a friendship." Yeah, that's cool.

The next day was my meeting with Tom and Mick. I couldn't imagine why they wanted to meet together with me.

"J-Dog, how's it going, man?" asked Tom.

"Yeah, I'm good," I replied.

As we walked into Mick's office, he greeted us. "How was the trip to Zurich?"

"Awesome!" I answered and sat down in the chair he pointed to.

After a few minutes of conversation about Zurich and a few pleasantries exchanged between Mick and Tom, Mick got to the purpose of our meeting.

"Jon," said Mick, "it seems like this has been a good year in FORM for you…would you say?"

"Oh, yeah, it's been great," I said, enthusiastically.

"We've watched you – and the others – grow spiritually so much," he observed.

"Yeah," I said, "it's amazing how different...how much....it's unbelievable how much God can do in such a short time," I paused. Neither of them said anything. I added, "My whole world is different...I mean...my direction...you know, the meaning of life. I can't imagine going through life without this experience. I'll never be the same...definitely!"

I was wondering where all this was going.

"We have an idea," Mick said, "and we would like you to pray about it."

I looked at Tom. He was smiling and shaking his head in affirmation. I could not have guessed what came next.

"We'd like to ask you to consider coming on staff here at the church," Mick said, "to work with university students."

I about went into cardiac arrest. Where did this come from? Man, I didn't see this coming. To work at this church....Holy...!

"Yeah," Tom added, "we reach students from the University of Sheffield, which is close. As you know, university students in this country don't have cars. The buses in the city don't run on Sundays because most people don't go to church, and all the shops are closed."

"We'd like to also target Sheffield Hallam University down on Ecclesall Road," said Mick. "We'd ask you to move down there and start a church for students from that campus. Would you pray about it?"

My mind was spinning. My first inclination was to talk to my parents.

Chapter Twenty-seven
Released and Ready

"Hellllllloooooooooooo," I said, as the picture of my parents came up on my computer screen.

"Hey, man, thanks for the Skype call," said my dad. "How is everything going? We got your letter to support partners about the Zurich trip. It sounds awesome!"

"Yeah, it was incredible," I said. God really showed up. We had so many good experiences. Our whole team really enjoyed it.

"Have you seen that girl again?" my mom asked and then turned to my dad, "What's her name?" My dad didn't remember, but my mom finally got it, "...Esther?"

"Yeah, she's fine. We had dinner together the other night," I responded. "It was good. She's nice."

"How's FORM?" my mom asked.

"Well, it's good," I answered, trying to figure out how to get into the next international, mind-boggling, historically significant, world-changing discussion, with at least a million ramifications for everyone in my family.

"How do I do this?" I thought. Deep breath. Little prayer. Oh heck....

"You'll never guess what happened," I said, with my best poker face. "They offered me a job on staff."

My parents looked enthused, and behind that I could see the struggle with the reality: "Will we ever see him again?"

"Yeah," I continued. "They want me to pray about planting a church among university students at Sheffield Hallam University," I paused. They seemed stunned. "I haven't decided anything yet. I wonder what you guys might think about it. It's a lot to think about."

It still didn't seem like they were ready to respond.

I continued, "It's complicated. I would come home for the summer and apply for a visa. I still won't be able to earn money, even after I get the visa. I'll have to raise my own support. They want me to move down in the area of the university. I'll have to find a room to rent. I won't be near the church, but I'll have an office there. I'll have to take the bus, walk, or get a bike. They want me for at least two years, if I take the job."

That was it. The whole bombshell. I knew it would be hardest on my mom. I held my breath when she spoke first.

"Is it something you think you really want to do?" she asked.

"I don't know right now. But I think, maybe. I am praying about it," I said.

My dad spoke while my heart stopped – it seemed. "What do you think God wants you to do?" he asked.

"I'm not totally sure," I said.

He continued, "Jon, you have got to do whatever God leads you to do. No matter how complicated or challenging, you have to follow your heart, follow God's leading."

"Well, I'm leaning a little this way," I said.

"You know, Jon," my dad was now going to get a little philosophical, I can always tell. "When you got invited to apply for FORM, I prayed like crazy you would apply, get accepted, and go. Then you went." He looked at my mom, who was wiping a few tears from her eyes. "We watched you on Skype, every few weeks, transformed before our very eyes." Now he got a little choked up. "You are every Christian father's dream come true – in spades!"

He paused. My mom was silent. I didn't know what to say. He continued, "There's an old saying, 'be careful what you pray for.' We prayed you would go. But we can't be selfish. You're a grown man. You've come to know God and have been equipped in ways I can't even imagine. Of course we miss you, but we can only be thrilled by this door God has opened up."

Yeah, my dad's a talker. Remember, he's a preacher by trade – before he became a consultant.

He had one more thing to say, "You know, when you open your life up to God, you do what the Bible says, 'Here am I, send me, send me.' You say that in obedience, but you don't get to choose where that is. And the adventure begins. You won't ever regret being faithful to God's call."

My dad has the right to say those things. That's what his life has been about. And my mom, too. She's followed him and always served God wherever his work took them. Yeah, they have the authentic authority to say that.

I felt, in that moment, I had the freedom to pray and follow God's lead. My parents loaned me to the university. Then they loaned me to go to FORM. All that was temporary. Today, they made it official. They released me to God. Thank God, I was finally ready.

After a couple of weeks, I knew that I knew. I'd be back in September. I was ready for FORM to come to a close. And

I wasn't ready. Both feelings were perfect. I was ready to take the next step. But I'd always continue FORM. I've learned to continue to learn. I can't believe this all happened in 10 months. I didn't become a student in order to do ministry. I learned ministry; and, in the process, became a life-long student!

Not all the FORM students were going into ministry. Most of them were going to follow other careers. But they would all be awesome Christians. They would be incredible volunteers in the churches they attend. If every church had students like this – with this training – it could change Christianity, wake it up! It could change the world.

I had seen Esther several more times in the last few weeks. I had this feeling…you think God can handle several miracles in my life all at once? I met her parents and her sisters. They were awesome people! Very cool!

I graduated from FORM in early June. My dad came over and brought another group of North Americans, just like he does every year. It was good to see him, even briefly. He said there was a lot of work on the farm to do. I had a summer job! I needed to go through whatever it took to get a visa.

I was leaving England. I was so different than when I came. God is good. Better than I expected. Better than I ever dreamed. You know what? I didn't sleep to forget anymore. I had experienced a spiritual wake-up call. I couldn't wait to face life. I wanted to start the next chapter. I just knew that in this next chapter, my next chapter, God would do great things in England. I just knew that. But I had no idea that the next chapter would lead me to impact North America, too!

Chapter Twenty-eight
Esther and Pop-Pop: Hello and Goodbye

"J-Dog?" Andy was behind me as I packed my bag.

"Hey, Andy, you leaving?" I asked.

"Yeah," he sighed. "We've got the car all packed. My parents are downstairs. I came to say good-bye."

He had tears in his eyes. I had a lump in my throat. I knew distance could never separate us. We were joined at the...heart...of Jesus...forever.

We hugged. "Love ya, man," I said, with a shaky voice.

"Love you, too," he said. "We'll keep in touch, right?"

"Absolutely," I affirmed. "Absolutely!"

We said good-bye and that was closure at the house. I went over to church and thanked Dan and Jude for a great year. I said good-bye to Mick, and then Tom. I knew I would see them again in a few short months. I couldn't believe it. I was coming back! Who would have ever guessed? Man, giving it over to God is a great adventure. You just never know. You just never know.

I spent the day with Esther. We were both glad I was coming back. She was going to come visit our place in Indiana in August. My dad met her when he was here with his group. He hugged her when he met her at church. I think, sometimes, parents know more, sooner, than their kids. How do they do that? Esther and I were going to Skype each day during the rest of June and July.

It was harder to say goodbye to Esther than I planned. There was definitely some chemistry there. I wondered where all this would lead. I wondered where my future would be. It didn't stress me out because, bottom-line, my future was with God. That means it would be okay. That doesn't mean it would always be easy, but it does mean it would be okay.

I took the train to Manchester Airport. It's amazing how familiar all this was. A year ago, I was a "foreigner." Now…well, I'm not a citizen of England, but I'm not a foreigner, either. My dad says I've become a world Christian – a citizen of God's Kingdom, with a heart for the world. He says I could end up anywhere. "Rule out nothing," he says. I was cool with that – I really was.

The trip home was uneventful. I brought a lot of clothes back to the U.S. But I left some things there. I was now a man with a foot in two worlds.

I was eager to get to work on the farm. I hadn't had a chainsaw in my hands for a long time. There was a lot of work to do. We were going to be clearing an 18-acre field filled with overgrown brush and trees. The previous owner had let it grow up. We had to clear it and spray all the stumps – by September, before I returned to England. The next spring, they would plant almost 10,000 trees, all in rows.

All summer, I worked from daylight to early afternoon. Then I'd take a lunch break. I'd make a sandwich and get on Skype and talk with Esther. She was back in Liverpool, living with her family and working. When it was 1 p.m. in Indiana, it was 6 p.m. in Liverpool – she was home from work. We talked every day.

After lunch, and an hour with Esther, I'd be back in the field until almost dark. I worked 15-hour days. My parents paid me. I also raised money through relatives and through people at the church. I got to see my friends several times: Nick, Nate, Mackenzie, and Tommy. I got to hang out with my cousin, David, too. That was cool!

It's funny how you drift apart, though. Nate and Tommy were going in a different direction, it seemed. We just weren't as close. Mackenzie – I wasn't sure – I hadn't been able to see him as much. Nick and I were still close. Nick seemed more interested in what God is doing in my life…and maybe his. Nick, Tommy, Nate, and I went to a three-day rock concert in Columbus, Ohio. It was awesome! What a party!

I started to work on my visa. I filled out lots of paperwork. It was a nightmare. It's amazing how much red tape the British Embassy can create. They don't make it easy to get in. I'm told embassies are like that, including the U.S.

My dad was swamped at work. He was developing something to help churches, called *Healthy Churches Thrive!* He and his staff had been working on pieces of this for years. They were getting ready to launch it. I looked at it. It's amazing how I could see the dynamics of church health because of my experience with FORM.

Esther came in August for a month. She got to meet my grandmother, on my mother's side, and all the family. Also, she got to meet Mom-Mom and Pop-Pop. Pop-Pop was not doing well. He was home for most of the summer, but had to go back to the hospital in late August.

Everyone loved Esther. I did, too. I mean love, as in…you know…a couple. Esther helped work in the field. Wow – what else could a guy ask for?

In late August, Esther went back to England. She moved back to Sheffield so we could continue to date, as I planted the church among students. Just after Esther left, Pop-Pop got worse. Dad and I laid hands on him. We looked at each other just before we prayed. We were thinking the same thing – without ever saying a word. We prayed, "Lord, heal Pop-Pop completely." We knew what we meant. Mom and Mom-Mom were there. I don't think they knew what we were thinking. We prayed he'd be perfectly healed, physically, or be perfectly healed by being taken home. God answered our prayer! He died. His funeral was just before I left for England. It was a victory celebration for a great Christian believer.

I returned to England and started planting a church. It was awesome, but extremely challenging work. I loved it! Esther and I continued our relationship and we started talking about the possibility of engagement. We were not in a hurry.

My university students go home for Christmas, so I went home to visit my family. The first Sunday I was home was the Sunday before Christmas. My mom was sick, so my dad and I went to church by ourselves. What happened next was, well, a miracle.

Chapter Twenty-nine
A Miracle at Pizza Hut

At Pizza Hut, we talked a lot about the Christian Movement – a talk we could not have had about a year before.

"Jon, you are not only my son, but you are like a colleague in mission," my dad said. Yeah, he had said that before.

He went on to say that he'd been "wrestling" with God for a year. He said Church Doctor Ministries was launching *Healthy Churches Thrive!* the next month, in January. He was excited, but couldn't get past the nagging feeling that once the church finished the Pilgrimage, and was healthy for mission, there ought to be something else – something more for a church to do – something like a second stage of a rocket.

He explained, "The first stage of a rocket going to, let's say Mars…that stage helps the rocket overcome gravity. Many churches are plagued by the 'country club' mentality that makes the church turn inward. That gravity keeps the church down. *Healthy Churches Thrive!* helps to escape that gravity. But every space vehicle has a booster rocket to propel it to Mars – or wherever – after it escapes gravity."

I could understand that. It made sense.

"I'm sure, Jon, that God has something in mind for this second stage. I just can't think of what it is. Do you have any idea?"

At the time, I just thought we were talking. I had no idea of the significance of the moment. It became another kairos moment – a time of the Lord: a "God moment." No question – God was at Pizza Hut. I said, "That's easy. Start something like FORM in North America...except make it different. Have one year just like FORM. But beyond discipleship training, do more training to help students become missionaries to North America, using 21st century strategies. Do the teaching, hands-on ministry experience, the mission trip, and the weekend excursions once a month. But also add training to be a missionary."

My dad was glued to the conversation. I was speaking, but it was like God was using my mouth, and my thoughts. Some might call it prophecy. It doesn't matter what you call it – God was all over it.

My dad said, "I wonder why I never thought about that?"

I said, "It doesn't matter. It's God."

He said, "That's brilliant!"

I continued, "And change it even more than FORM. Everything God does is about multiplication, right?"

"Absolutely," my dad said. I think he knew where this was going.

"You need to have a second year of FORM training for students who would like to become FORM leaders."

My dad said, "Since it focuses on training missionaries to North America, why don't we call it SEND...SEND North America?" SEND is the New Testament word for 'mission.' You know, Jesus said, 'As the Father has sent me, so I SEND you.'"

"Exactly!" I said. "Look, you start with a SEND unit here in Indiana. At the end of the next June, you graduate the students. Let's say six or so of them go on to train to be leaders, and take the second year. They come back a second year and learn to be leaders and are trained while the next group takes the first year. The leader of SEND works with the leader students and disciples them through on-the-job training. Then when they graduate, they're placed in churches that are SEND-ready."

"Churches become SEND-ready," my dad said, "through *Healthy Churches Thrive!*"

"That's right," I continued, "and now these churches have a SEND unit. And in the second year, they start producing leaders."

"And, meanwhile," my dad jumps in, "We develop a SEND North American network site, which is a recruiting mechanism through the Web to keep attracting 20-somethings who are interested in the SEND training."

"You get it," I said, "and the whole thing multiplies. And you have a movement of on-fire missionaries."

"And having a SEND unit at a church, each and every year, year after year," dad said, "will keep the missionary climate going at that church and reach people for Christ through that church, utilizing the students."

"Yeah," I said, "and most churches seem to be getting 'older.' You know, fewer young people. But what better way to reach more young adults than through a group of fired-up young adults being trained, year after year, at the church?"

"Not only that," Dad continued, "after a while, each church with a SEND unit will be training up these students, and some will become future staff – just as St. Thomas called you to be a church planter. It's like every church has its own 'farm club'."

Dad thought for a minute. Everything was silent. I saw his wheels turning. "You know," he said, "what if we targeted a SEND unit to be around 25 students? The tuition would cover the cost of the SEND leader's salary, curriculum, and other costs. It wouldn't cost the church anything extra to have a SEND unit."

He paused to think through the last step. I couldn't guess what was coming.

"Then, as for the students, they should not pay for their tuition. They should raise it, say, from 10 families. You raised your support for England because you had to. But what if that was, continually, part of SEND? It would take the cost burden off the student, teach them to be accountable to their support partners, and they would report to their 10 families each month. The 25 students would report to 10 families about what they are learning, just as you reported to Mom and me. The students would become "teachers" about missionary strategies and discipleship to 10 families each. That's 250 families each month! These families would be learning and probably sharing it with their churches. We would be spreading the movement even further!"

I said, "Brilliant!"

Dad said, "Sounds like something a British person would say: 'Brilliant!'"

Chapter Thirty
Think about God

Think about what God has done in two and a half years:

> Rescued me as a directionless student in my last year of university.
>
> Moved me to England.
>
> Discipled and equipped me through FORM.
>
> Gave me purpose for life.
>
> Called me to be a student worker with British university students.
>
> Introduced me to a beautiful, young woman from Liverpool, who is now my wife.
>
> Birthed SEND North America in a Pizza Hut.
>
> Began a movement of North American young adults to revitalize churches and lay the ground work for revival.

Don't tell me God can't do something in your life. I promise you: He can…and will!

J-Dog

What's Next for You?

Self-Reflection Tool
Is God Launching You on a Journey?

(Scale 1-10; 1=not much, 10=oh yeah)

Circle your number

Are you restless about your direction in life?	1 2 3 4 5 6 7 8 9 10
Are you unsure about why you are here?	1 2 3 4 5 6 7 8 9 10
Do you want to make a difference in this world?	1 2 3 4 5 6 7 8 9 10
Have you wondered if God has something special for you?	1 2 3 4 5 6 7 8 9 10
Have you ever thought about going deeper in your faith life?	1 2 3 4 5 6 7 8 9 10
Are you a relational person, who cares about others?	1 2 3 4 5 6 7 8 9 10
Are you unclear about who you are?	1 2 3 4 5 6 7 8 9 10
Would you like to see the fun side of Christianity?	1 2 3 4 5 6 7 8 9 10
Does experiencing an adventure excite you?	1 2 3 4 5 6 7 8 9 10
Do you think God could use you to help change the world?	1 2 3 4 5 6 7 8 9 10

If you scored a total of 70 or more, check out
www.sendnorthamerica.com

ABOUT THE AUTHOR

Kent R. Hunter serves as guide to the awesome team that leads SEND North America, a young adult training movement committed to changing the world. He is the author of many books focusing on church discipleship. His most recent book--*Who Broke My Church?*--is now available at Amazon.com.

Kent says his reason for being on this earth is to help Christians and churches become more effective for the Great Commission, to make disciples of all peoples. He recognizes that America is the third largest mission field in the world (behind China and India). His passion is to come alongside pastors and church leaders to provide encouragement, direction, focus, and turn challenges into opportunities for mission through the local church.